Punky

The Paul Randall Story

To Carlos
Hope you enjoy the book.
Best wishes
Paul.

Paul Randall & Neil Palmer

Punky

The Paul Randall Story

DB
PUBLISHING

This edition published in Great Britain in 2013 by DB Publishing, an imprint of JMD Media.

ISBN 9781780910277

Printed and bound by Copytech (UK) Limited, Peterborough.

Contents

Neil Palmer

Neil Palmer is a writer who hails originally from Cardiff but now resides in Bristol with his wife and two grown up children. *'PUNKY'* is Neil's fifth book to date. Others have included the popular *Derby Days* and *When Rugby Was Rugby*. Neil has also contributed to various publications and football websites over the years.

Neil and Paul first became friends during the research of Neil's *Bristol Derby Days* book and it was Neil who Paul turned to when he decided to set his own life down in print.

Outside of writing, Neil is a keen follower of Cardiff City and Bristol Rugby Club.

I first met Paul Randall in the winter of 2007. I was in the process of writing *Bristol Derby Days*, a book about the Bristol Derby between City and Rovers. When I drew up my list of ex-Rovers players to speak to, Paul's was the first name on the paper.

Paul Randall

Although not a Rovers or City fan (my allegiances lie across the water in Cardiff), I knew he was still loved by the 'Gas Heads' and loathed by the 'red side' of Bristol, as he always seemed to score against City. I was also aware of the 'supermarket kid' tag that seemed to follow him around his career since that FA Cup game against Southampton all those years ago. Knowing that Paul left the game early, I wondered what sort of man would greet me as I walked towards his front door that November night. Would he be bitter at having to drop down to non-league at the young age of 28? And would he be sick and tired of the references to supermarkets? He welcomed me in, and we sat and talked football for hours. I don't think I have met a more engaging and down-to-earth man. When the book was released, I really got to see the love that is still there for Paul from the 'blue' half of Bristol. I also found a level of respect towards Paul shown by the red half as well.

Paul never said no to a photo or a signing at various events. And the reception he got from the Rovers faithful brought a lump to my throat, as it showed he was not forgotten. We talked about doing a book, and in 2011 we finally decided to write it after the tragic death of his sister Vinny. The book has been part of a healing process for him and his family.

It's been a pleasure to spend time with the Randall Family. Paul's mum, June, and dad, Ken, are wonderful people and have helped me greatly, as have sisters Lorraine, and Gail. Fil, Mark and Kelly have also put up with me arriving on a Friday night and spending hours with Paul, and for that I cannot thank them enough. As for Paul, it has been a privilege to work with you on this book and to hopefully tell the story of one of Bristol Rovers' greats, and one of life's gentlemen.

Neil Palmer

Acknowlegements

I first spoke to Neil when he rang and asked if I would do a chapter for the *Bristol Derby Days* book. When the book came out, myself and several of the other players featured did a few book signings. Neil asked me if I had ever thought about doing an autobiography. I had, but I never thought it would become a reality. Thank you Neil, you have become a friend for life. I would also like to thank Neil's wife Sally for letting Neil out every other Friday evening to talk football. Sally and my wife Fil don't realise they have a lot in common; they both dislike football, so it must have been our obvious good looks that they fell for.

My mum, dad and sisters have always been there throughout my career and through my life. They have all watched me from an early age and, between them, they must have watched nearly every game I have played, from school to the end of my career. Dad has always kept me on my toes, making sure I trained after work when I was first at Glastonbury so that I always had that extra edge over my opponents. He has always believed in me throughout the bad times and the good, so thank you dad for being at my side.

Another big thank you goes to my lovely family – Fil, Mark and Kelly. Fil has her own career in management and hates football, so Saturday has always been my day for it. Many a time I have returned from a game to describe how I scored a hat-trick, and to be honest, I might as well have been talking double Dutch. So thank you for putting up with my football obsession. My children Mark and Kelly are now grown up and have made Fil and I very proud parents.

Can I also thank Dave "titch" Titchner for some wonderful photographs from my career, Tony Pulis, Ian Holloway and everybody who wrote something for the book. Particularly the fans of the various teams I played for. I am very touched by the kind words they have all written. I would also like to thank Steve and his team at DB Publishing and Amanda Nicholls for making the book happen. Credit also goes to Colin Burgess at Stoke City, Keith Brookman at Bristol Rovers, Dave Linney at Yeovil Town, Ned Vaught at Bath City and Mike Sadler at Glastonbury, also Mike Jay and Stephen Byrne for their incredible knowledge of 'The Gas'. Thank you all for helping with this story.

I would like to thank the late Georgie Petherbridge – a true Bristol Rovers legend. George was manager of the Somerset County team I played in at youth and senior level; he believed in me and kept on to Rovers to take a look at me. So thank you George for playing a big part in my career. And finally, to every supporter who has ever chanted my name. I gave you memories but you have given me so many more…Thank you.

Foreword

Ian Holloway

It's a great honour to be asked to write a foreword for such a Bristol Rovers legend as Paul Randall. I was a boy, stood in the Tote End when Paul 'Punky' Randall made his debut for Rovers just after being plucked from a supermarket job. He was playing non-league football and was thrown straight into the first team. What a story! A real life *Roy (Paul) of the Rovers*, literally. Bang! What an amazing impact the long-haired, skinny lad made. He was a scoring sensation and instant crowd favourite; someone who gave hope to every lad who had aspirations of becoming a footballer. At the time, I was at Rovers in the youth system and found him totally inspirational. It is possible, you can do it!

Like a duck to water, he leapt division after division and made it look so easy. Just when you thought the story couldn't get any better, higher league clubs came calling and Rovers were forced to sell him. Knowing Paul as well as I do, I am happy to say that he has never changed from that very same lad. He continued to have a glittering career and remained grounded and forever a Gas Head! He epitomised the Bristol Rovers spirit and in my opinion, there is not a bigger Bristol Rovers legend than 'Punky'. It was a pleasure to play with him and, as a Gas Head myself, a joy to watch him score for the best team in Bristol.

Ian Holloway ('Ollie')

Foreword

Tony Pulis

I was thrilled to be asked to write a foreword for Punky's book. I have known Paul a long time and I'm sure the book will make interesting reading for any football fan – after all, it's a real inspirational story of a lad plucked from non-league to play at the highest level in the game.

I remember when Paul first arrived at Bristol Rovers. They were a very good club with some decent youngsters at the time and Paul fitted right in, on and off the field. He quickly became a fans' favourite with his devastating pace and eye for a goal, and who will ever forget his performance in the FA Cup against Southampton, in a match that would go on to change his life? Manager Bobby Campbell came to me one day after training and said that the club had received a bid for Paul and asked me what I thought. I told Bobby that it would be very difficult to keep hold of him, and whoever replaced him would have to fill some very big boots. The club sold him to Stoke City and the £180,000 fee is testimony to how good Paul was. At Stoke he won over the supporters by scoring again as they won promotion to the top flight.

He is a fantastic lad and was never any trouble for me in my roles as coach and teammate. Looking back, I'm proud to have been there at the start of his career and stayed friends to this day, even though I used to run him ragged in pre-season.

Tony Pulis

Introduction

I wanted to open my autobiography by recalling an event that changed both my family and me forever; the death of my sister Vinny. I felt it was important, as it was this event that prompted me to sit down with Neil Palmer and write my story. I had been told by friends, as most ex-footballers are, that I should write a book, but I never really thought I would do it. But after something like this, I felt a real passion to put my life on paper. The book is not a birds, booze and gambling-type book – it's just the story of a local lad and his rise to the top, and how important his family was in that rise. I found this opening very difficult to write but I'm very proud of getting it down on paper. This is that terrible event.

Was that the telephone ringing or was I dreaming? I eventually opened my eyes as the last ring finished. I looked at the clock at the side of my bed and it told me it was 4.30am on Sunday morning, 11 July 2009. A start to a day that myself and my family will never forget.

I picked up the phone and dialled 1471 to see who had rung. I thought I recognised the number as my middle sister Lavinia's. There was no message left, so I put the phone down and lay back in bed. The phone ringing had woken my wife, Filomena, and she asked who had called. I said I thought it was Vinny (that's what the family name is for Lavinia) but I couldn't be sure. Within a minute, the phone went again; it was Nathan, the partner of Vinny's daughter Maria. They were both babysitting Vinny's other son Tom, as she had gone out to a party in her local village. He said he had a policeman at the house and that he wanted to talk to me. I don't know what was going through my mind, but I was not expecting what I was about to be told.

'Are you Paul Randall?' the policeman asked.

'Yes,' I replied.

'We don't usually do this over the phone,' he said, 'but Lavinia has been involved in a hit-and-run and has life-threatening injuries.'

He asked if could I get the family together and go straight to the hospital. I could feel my heart racing and all sorts of awful thoughts were going through my mind. Fil had heard everything and started to get upset. We are a very close family. How was I going to tell my mum and dad and my other two sisters? This was going to break their hearts. I got dressed and drove over to my younger sister Gail and her husband John. I banged on their door but there was no reply. Gail eventually came to the door and I could see the surprise on her face. I explained everything to her about what had happened. I have never seen a face lose its colour so quickly and her shoulders just sank. We had one problem and that was that our sister Lorraine and her husband Stuart were in France on holiday with their friends Billy Jones and Julie Culliford. We tried to contact her on her mobile but got no reply, so we left a message for her to ring us as soon as possible. I had been given a telephone number for the Bath Royal United Hospital; Gail phoned and told them who we were and what had happened. They said they had a lady fitting the description we gave and again we were told she had life-threatening injuries, and to get there as soon as possible. But before that we had the unenviable task of telling our mum and dad, who live in the town of Street a few miles away.

My God; how were we going to break the news? How would they react? Gail and John changed and they drove over to mum and dad's. I told them to wait outside until I got there. I felt it was my duty and responsibility, as the oldest, to break the news to them. I nipped home to see if Fil was okay, as she was phoning Tesco – where she worked as a store manager. She said she would rather stay at home while I went over. Bless her, I don't think she could face it. As I was driving over, I was getting these awful, bad thoughts; was this happening or was it a bad dream? Knocking on the door, I think we were all in shock. Dad answered the door in his pyjamas as mum was still in bed. Standing at the front door, I told him what had happened. He slumped against the wall shouting 'Vinny, Vinny, Vinny'. Gail picked him up and cuddled him while I went into the bedroom. I will always remember what my mum said as I was standing in the doorway.

I said, 'Mum, Vinny has been involved in an accident.'

Mum said, 'now what's she done?'

If anything was going to go wrong it would happen to Vin, she was one of those people. I told mum it was more serious than that and explained what had happened. Mum said later that while I was explaining to her, it seemed like everything was in slow motion. This was the hardest thing Gail and I have ever had to do in our lives – telling our mum and dad that one of their daughters had been involved in a hit-and-run and had life-threatening injuries. I remember thinking that after all I had said, there were no tears. Was it the shock? In between all the commotion, John made a cup of tea for mum and dad while they got changed. We decided that John and Gail would take mum and dad to the hospital while I picked Fil up on the way.

When we got to the hospital, Vinny's children Maria and Tom were there with Nathan, having come up with the police. We were taken into a private room and told by a nurse that a doctor would be along shortly to talk to us. They said that with the severity of Vinny's injuries, they would have expected her to be dead and would have stopped treatment if it had not been for a reaction by Vinny – to pull her oxygen tube from her mouth. So because of this they were going to take her to Frenchay Hospital in Bristol for a brain scan and an operation. The doctor asked if we had any questions. There were probably hundreds, but at the time your mind goes blank with all the information you have just been told. I think mum and dad asked a few but I could not tell you what they were. We asked if we could see her before she went to Frenchay. Only mum dad, Gail and myself went into see her as nobody felt up to it, which was understandable.

Mum and Gail went first; then I went in with dad. Poor Vinny; tubes and machines bleeping everywhere. I remember thinking, 'look at her lovely blonde hair covered in blood, she won't be happy with that.' She was always well dressed and very pretty. Was this to be the last time I would ever see her? We went back to the room and the doctor came in and told us they were ready to go to Frenchay. By this time my son Mark and daughter Kelly had arrived and Tom had fallen asleep on Fil's shoulder. I was talking to Mark, Kelly and Nathan in the corridor, when all of a sudden they wheeled Vinny out. The look of horror on their faces and seeing them so upset is something I will never forget. As the ambulance pulled away, Gail's phone rang and it was Lorraine. Gail told her what had happened and Lorraine screamed and hung up. Seconds later, her husband Stuart rang back and asked how bad it really was. Gail said it was really bad, and they had to come home. Lorraine and Stuart left France virtually straight away. With the combination of driving and the ferry, it took them 16 hours to get home with Billy and Julie, who said they would help with the driving; what true friends they were. Mark and Kelly took Tom home to get some clothes so he could sleep at our house that night, and everybody else went to Frenchay, except for me and Fil. We went back to mum and dad's house to let the dog out for a toilet; in all this, life goes on.

When we got to Frenchay, Gail went off to find out where Vinny was. Gail came back to tell us she was undergoing an operation, so we went to the restaurant in the hospital and sat about, making ridiculous small talk. The operation to remove blood clots on the brain and to address other serious injuries lasted six hours. After the operation, Vinny was taken into intensive care where she was put on a life support machine and made comfortable. We were taken into a waiting room; from where we could go and see her two at a time. When I got to go in and see her, reality really sunk in and I stood there, helpless. There was my beautiful sister, lying there, surrounded by tubes wired to machines, her head shaved and staples everywhere. 'Please wake me up', I thought, but there was nothing else we could do, so we were all told to go home and rest.

On the Sunday morning, Lorraine and Stuart got back and we met them at Frenchay. We sat about the waiting room, taking it in turns to sit with Vinny. Monday was the same; Fil had to go back to work so the rest of us sat with Vin. On the Tuesday, the doctor decided to drop Vinny's medication to try and see if she would come round but they got no reaction. Then came the shocking news, as the doctor told us that if she came round she would be brain damaged, and blind because of the damage to her eye sockets. Deep down, we all feared the worst.

On Wednesday there was no change, until I got a phone call at 11.45pm. It was mum; she told me the neurosurgeon had decided to do another brain scan and found a huge blood clot that was causing too much pressure on the brain. He also needed to take a piece of skull away to help the brain. Mum told me he needed to operate but to prepare for the worst if it did not work. I could not get back to sleep as I paced around the house, thinking of Vinny.

Thursday morning at 3.15am, the phone rang and it was Mum again. She explained that the surgeon had tried everything he could and asked us to get the family together, as mum and dad had agreed to turn the life support machine off sometime that day. My heart sank; I was numb. How brave were mum and dad to make that decision? They had been so strong through it all. We all met outside my house and took the final journey to Frenchay Hospital. We were taken to a family room in the intensive care unit and waited for the doctor to talk to us. They told us that they were slowly going to reduce Vinny's medication and turn off her life support machine. The doctors, surgeons and nurses were brilliant to us all throughout the ordeal. We waited until they had Vinny comfortable then mum, Gail, John, Maria, Nathan, Stuart, and sons James and myself went in to say our goodbyes. A chaplain gave her the last rites they switched the life support machine off at 2.30pm and we sat with her as she fell asleep for the last time. It was too much for Dad and Lorraine – they went in to say their goodbyes later. I rang Fil, Mark and Kelly to let them know the sad news and they were, like us, all heartbroken.

We all went back to Lorraine's house and just sat there talking about Vinny and our memories of her. I am not trying to be the big man but I have not cried properly to this day. I get upset when I see members of my family crying and there is nothing I can do to stop the hurt they are feeling. What I have realised after a huge tragedy like this, is that when you are given an opportunity in life, grab it with both hands and make the best of it and be grateful to be so lucky. Treasure your family and say you love them every day.

Paul Randall

Chapter One

From Aldershot with Love

I made my debut in this world (sorry, old habits die hard) on the 16 February 1958. My mum, June, told my dad, Ken, that their first-born was definitely on the way. So being the proud expectant father my dad obviously was, he got on the bus with my mum and her little brown suitcase that she had packed for this moment, and they set off for Sefton General Hospital in Liverpool.

Being a typical scouser who loved his football, on arriving at the hospital he helped mum off the bus, gave her a kiss and proceeded to get back on the bus, as this was a Saturday and he was playing that afternoon for local team Florence Albion. So off he went, mouthing the words 'I love you' through the window of the bus. He apparently came to see us Sunday afternoon, after celebrating becoming a father and a 4–0 win for the Albion. So as you can see, football has been part of my life from the very start.

My mum and dad are a wonderful mixture of two different worlds, and I have the British Army to thank for getting them together – although how they have stayed together puzzles me and my sisters to this day. I suppose they just fit together perfectly. My mum was born in Dar es Salaam, which used to be the capital of Tanzania on the east coast of Africa. Her father was a merchant seaman who landed in the port and loved it so much that he jumped ship and stayed. He met my grandmother there; she was working in service at the time. She was originally from Glastonbury and her family had moved to Africa, due to her father being one of the first white hunters to operate there. They got married and my grandfather got a job in government. And by all accounts, they had a wonderful life.

Mum's parents were really old-school colonial types – never any cuddles for the children and it was all very stiff upper lip. I remember them when they retired and moved back to Glastonbury, as they looked after my sister Lorraine and me. We would watch the TV and when it was finished for the evening, the BBC used to play the national anthem (our cue to go to bed) and granddad made sure we all stood to attention while the anthem played. So they were never really what you would call warm grandparents, but they certainly prepared me if I was ever to play for England!

Mum spent most of her childhood in boarding school, as did her brother Richard, while her parents travelled around with her father's government work. Mum says her friends were her family in the boarding school and although to people on the outside looking in, it appeared that she had a very privileged upbringing, I think, deep down, she missed the love and affection of a close family. I guess that's why she is so affectionate to me and my sisters and our families to this day. I think she never wanted us to feel anything but love and support growing up; something she achieved in spades.

Mum came back to England with her family in 1954, aged 17. Her family wanted her to go to a finishing school in Brighton to become a stenographer then return to East Africa to work for one of the big oil companies, but she had other ideas, and on a stroll through Brighton with her brother, she went into the Army Recruitment Centre and joined the Women's Royal Army Corps. She was always good at sport throughout her life and the army obviously brought that out in her, as she represented her regiment in athletics on many occasions. One such occasion brought her, aged 18, to the Aldershot Athletics stadium for a meeting and that's where she first set eyes on a very handsome scouser called Ken (he made me write that).

Ken Randall, my dad, is a real man's man. He was brought up in the Dingle area of Toxteth, Liverpool, where he lived with his mum, dad, two brothers and a sister. His father worked in a warehouse while his mum looked after the kids. It was a tough upbringing with not a lot of money about, but Toxteth back then had a real community feel about the place, where everybody looked after each other. I have good memories of my dad's father; he was called Jack and reminded me of Norman Wisdom. He was the sweetest man you could ever meet. Some of my earliest memories are of holding his hand while we watched my dad play football for St Christopher's on a Sunday morning.

Dad loved sport, especially football, and I'm sure he would have made it as a player if he had been encouraged as a youngster, but in those days you just went out to work to bring money in. He played for various local teams as a big centre-half and also had games for Aldershot Town and Everton Reserves, but he says he just wasn't good enough to make it to the top. When I look at him and imagine him as a young player, I think he would have scared the shit out of me when I was playing. Not becoming a footballer never made dad bitter, I think it just encouraged him to support me in everything I did, and boy did he do that. He never missed a football match I played in throughout my career; he would travel all over the country to see me and it meant so much to me to know he was in the stands, watching. Everybody knew Ken Randall and even today when I visit any of my old clubs or meet up with any old player, the first thing they ask is; 'how's your dad, Paul?'

Dad joined the army in 1954, where he became a motor mechanic, and after six months he became a physical training instructor. How he managed that career jump only he knows. Anyway, that's what brought him to the Aldershot Stadium, where he was setting out the hurdles for the lads he was instructing. He looked up and saw what he described as 'the most beautiful girl in the world' (soppy bugger). They were married on 10 November 1956 and moved into dad's parents' already crowded house until dad was demobbed from the army in 1957. Mum says she learnt everything from her mother-in-law, as up until that time she couldn't even think about how to run a house. It was obviously a long way from having servants but that's what love does for you. They got their first flat in Ashfield Road, Liverpool, and that's where I was born and where my sister Lorraine was born.

We lived in Liverpool for three years and then moved down to Glastonbury, where mum's parents had retired. Dad got a job as a lorry driver and I think they moved so it would give us all a better quality of life. We moved into a tiny cottage, which sounds idyllic but it had no water or electricity, and all for the price of five shillings a week rent. So it wasn't long before we got ourselves on the council list, and boy, did we go through that list! Growing up, I must have lived in 10 council houses from 1962 to 1985. My mum used to move in, decorate the property then decide she was bored with living in it, and off to the council offices she would go. Next thing we knew, she would tell us we were moving. I swear I must have lived in every street in Glastonbury. I only wish she had been my agent when I was playing as she would have moved me to so many clubs that I would have earned a fortune in transfer fees.

I have three sisters; Lorraine, Gail and Vinny, and I wouldn't change them for the world. Being the eldest, I felt very protective towards them. When I was aged about six, I decided I was going to be a hairdresser. Now, anybody who has seen photos of me in my playing career will realise that I have no idea about hairstyles; my perm at Bristol Rovers will confirm that. Anyway, I got some scissors from the kitchen, and a willing customer in the shape of Lorraine and off I went, cutting her long hair. Although with every chop of her hair I think Loraine lost faith in my ability, I only stopped when there was no more hair to cut. Mum and dad returned home to find Lorraine hiding behind the TV, too afraid to show off her new 'hairstyle'. When she did, my career as a hairdresser ended – with me getting a slap on the arse from my dad and sent off to bed.

I can also remember Lorraine asking me, when I was about 14, if I could show her how to throw a punch. So, I got my boxing gloves out and proceeded to show her. First punch was textbook – it stopped inches from her nose, as did the second, but the third punch did not go as I had planned as it landed straight on her nose and knocked her out. I was mortified as I saw her fall back against the wall and slide down it. I ripped off the gloves and started slapping her face shouting, 'Lorraine! Lorraine!' She came to after a few seconds, although it felt like an eternity. I screamed at her, 'don't tell mum and dad!' and to her credit, she never did.

Lorraine often gave as good as she got and I remember on one occasion she got me back. We were at St Benedict's School and I must have been about 12. I was playing cricket with my mates when Lorraine came over and asked if she could play. I told her to shove off, but to my amazement my mates said let her play. Eventually I gave in and let her bowl at me. As she ran up, I thought I'd hit her for six and that would teach her to play a lad's game. But she bowled a killer ball that Freddie Flintoff would have been proud of, and smashed my wicket while I was left sweeping the air – much to the amusement of my mates. So I threw the bat down and stormed off, which made me look even more of an idiot and threw my mates and Lorraine into hysterics. My sister Lorraine was a real tomboy; there was only 18 months between us and growing up we were inseparable. Almost like a mini mum and dad, helping to look after our other sisters Vinny and Gail. She was also brilliant at sport and I'm sure that's why my mates did not mind her hanging around with us; she really was one of the lads. Together, we seemed to win every sporting event at school and we held titles in athletics and tennis. Sister Vinny was also a good athlete, breaking various records at school, and I'm sure both her and Lorraine could have gone on to great things in sport if they had wanted to.

Vinny was a real character – very similar to dad and I think that's why they clashed so often. If there was trouble about, it was usually Vinny at the centre. She was very strong-willed and not afraid to speak her mind, which was different to the laidback approach that Lorraine and myself adopted. Having said that, the room lit up when she entered it; she really was the life spark of our family and I think it's true to say that a little bit of all of us died when she was so tragically taken from us.

As for the youngest, Gail, we certainly did her no favours at school. The name Randall had become synonymous with sporting achievement at St Dunstan's, so when she arrived and the sports master said to her, 'ahh another Randall – and what do you do on the sports field?' The fact that she replied, 'smoke', says everything about Gail's sporting prowess.

Those days when we were kids really were idyllic, and I know people often think of their childhood like that but ours truly was. We were lucky there were no cars in the road, and we would play in fields and climb trees and use our imaginations. We really were like the four musketeers with an, 'all for one and one for all' attitude, and that's how we lived as a family. We did everything together. We would watch TV and all have our own places like the comedy series *The Royale Family*, with me usually lying on the front room floor.

We never had much as kids but it never bothered us, in fact, I don't think we would have been happier if we were millionaires. My mum and dad always worked hard to give us what they could. I remember our first holiday. I was 19 and had just signed for Bristol Rovers. We all piled in to my dad's Austin A40, together with our dog Honey – I don't know how we ever all got in, let alone tackled some of those hills on the way to our destination (a caravan in Weymouth). But we did it.

Looking back, those childhood days shaped my life for the better and I have mum, dad, Lorraine, Vinny and Gail to thank for that. I'm sure the freedom we had as kids and the strong sense of family gave me the confidence that would prove so valuable to me in my career.

Chapter Two

The Road to Glastonbury

Football was always important to me as a kid. And it was the opportunity to play the game rather than watch it that I craved. Don't get me wrong; I loved watching the game on the BBC's *Match of The Day* or ITV's *The Big Match*. I would be so excited watching great players of the 1960s and 70s performing on TV. Being a Liverpool fan, if I got to go back to the city with dad to visit relatives, there was always a trip to Anfield thrown in. I would be in awe of the place, the singing and the atmosphere, and to see legendary players like Ian St John and Kevin Keegan play was a joy for a young lad. I would just look around and dare to dream about whether I could ever play there.

But nothing ever felt better than kicking a ball around with my mates, or having dad show me some trick that would improve my game. I would spend hour upon hour practicing outside the house, knocking the ball against the wall from one foot to the other. I remember dad put a screw in a tennis ball and tied a piece of string to it, and told me only to kick it with my left foot. This I did over and over again until my foot got strong and as good as my right – I couldn't wait to show him when I had mastered it.

Dad was, and still is, a massive influence on my career and life; he encouraged me and always told me that I would make it one day. I know I was his son, but he could be brutally honest with me and always told me if I had a good or poor game, which was good for me. He always had my best interests at heart. He knew just how to handle me, particularly when it came to discipline, and although I never caused him or mum any trouble growing up, he knew what made me tick.

I remember being about 12 and playing football with my mates. I think I hit a neighbour's window after being told by dad not to play around these particular houses. Anyway, like most parents, dad found out and I was grounded for the night. So there I am, sat in my bedroom, feeling sorry for myself, when the doorbell goes and it's my mates – asking if I can go out. Dad opens the door and I am listening on the upstairs landing when he tells them I'm grounded. Just before they leave they ask, 'Mr Randall, can we borrow Paul's football?' and he replies, 'of course' and gets it from the downstairs cupboard, and off they go up the road with me crying looking at them from my bedroom window. I never played around those houses again or hit another window after that.

My schooldays are also remembered with affection. I was a good student and always in the top sets even though I could play the fool and entertain my mates. In fact, my impressions of certain stars of the day like Mick Jagger, Max Wall and Frankie Howard were legendary in the school corridors until some teacher – usually Mr Price, who was welsh and had a booming voice – would shout, 'Randall stop larking about.'

Although Mr Price was a good bloke, we never really saw eye-to-eye when it came to sport. He took us for PE and in one lesson he decided that we would play, as he put it, 'God's own game', in other words, rugby. So I was dispatched to play full back due to my speed rather than my enthusiasm. Within minutes, the odd-shaped ball came to me and I grabbed it and ran for the opposition posts, but then WHACK – I was crashed to the floor by somebody's elbow. I got up, looked at Pricey who was refereeing the game and said, 'Mr Price, that is the first and last time I ever play rugby, sir', and with that I walked off the pitch towards the changing room; with a detention to go with it if I remember rightly.

Another teacher I remember at school was Arthur Dunford – he really believed in me as a footballer and he would often tell me that I could make it as a player. Mr Dunford was a lovely man, he loved talking about the war and I would always say at the start of his lessons, 'what was it like in the war, sir?', and off he would go, telling us every detail, and the next thing you knew, the lesson was over. But above all that, he followed my career and genuinely believed I would be a football player which ironically, was the complete opposite of the careers officer, who asked me to leave the office after I told him I wanted to be a footballer! I played in the football team throughout school, from infants to seniors, and I always scored goals, but I really started to bang them in when I played for local village side, Charlton Mackerel. I was about 12 years old and I would score 100 goals a season; we were a great team and would regularly beat opponents 20–0. I was also picked to play for the local representative side, Mid-Somerset. I remember winning one game 4–3; I scored two goals and my mate from school, Paul Cove, got the other two. We had to stand up in assembly and receive the applause from the school, which I have to admit made me feel very proud. In fact, I still see Paul today and we still talk about that. I found that playing at a higher-level came naturally as I scored goals for the representative side on a regular basis. I loved travelling around the South West with the side and I really did feel it would not be long before I got a trial somewhere, even at that young age.

As I said before, I always preferred playing to watching football but I would always go down to support my local side, Glastonbury, in the Western League. Glastonbury's golden years were in the late 40s and early 50s when they won the Western League title twice and were runners-up twice. They also reached the FA Cup first round in 1951, losing 2–1 at home to Exeter City in front of 4,000 fans. There had not been much recent success when I was a kid, but it was my local side and I loved going. Glastonbury's ground was called The Abbey Park, which was a great place with its own little stand on the one side. It also had its own duck pond next door where the supporters always told the referee he was going if he had a bad game. There would be about 100 supporters at the games and I remember watching players like Peter Bolton, Len Beale, Tony Rice, Dave Noake and Vic Barney, formerly of Bristol Rovers. And although these players were not well known outside of Glastonbury, they were famous as far as I was concerned.

The great thing about small teams like Glastonbury was that at half-time me and my mates would go behind the goal and have a kick-about, which was really a chance to show off to the supporters, although the groundsman would watch us like a hawk if we strayed onto the Abbey pitch! I went on my own one Saturday to see a reserve game when I was 13 years old. I was stood behind the goal when one of the Glastonbury coaches came over to me and asked me, 'Are you Ken Randall's son?' I said that I was and he asked me if I had any boots and if I wanted to play. Well, I sprinted home, burst into the house and blurted out to my mum; 'I need my boots, where are my boots? I am playing for Glastonbury today – quick, where's my boots?' without even drawing a breath.

I got back to the ground and went into the Nissen hut that passed for the team changing rooms, and there I stood amongst the regular players with my Glastonbury kit on – which was about ten times too big for me and weighed a ton. I was introduced to the team and I was told I was to be the substitute. I was in dreamland – to me at that age it was like being at Wembley Stadium or Anfield, ready to go out in front of 60,000. I couldn't believe it was happening to me. I never got on the pitch that day but I didn't care. The coach said to me that they had heard about me and would I like to come again. So there I was, 13 years old and playing for Glastonbury Reserves against men, hoping it would not be long before professional clubs would notice this scrawny youngster.

Chapter Three

Never Give Up

I made my debut for Glastonbury Reserves a week later at Ilminster FC, coming on for 20 minutes. I can't remember the score but I know I did okay; in fact, a friend of mine, Merv Clark, who was a first-team player at the time and was playing in that game, claims I played a perfect one-two, which set up a goal for him. I was obviously getting known locally, especially playing at a higher level at such a young age, when I suddenly got an offer from Bristol City to join them for two-week trial.

The offer came about through a neighbour who was Bristol City player Peter Spiring's dad. Peter was a Glastonbury lad and his dad told scout Jock Rae about me. Jock, who is sadly no longer with us, was a wonderful man and a bit of a legend in the South West for the local talent he produced for City. He was a tough old Scot, who looked like Sir Matt Busby. Dad took me up to Bristol and I felt like it was a million miles away, even though it was only about 30. It was the summer holidays and I stayed in digs in Ashton near the ground with some other lads. It was a bit daunting for all of us, considering we were all about 13 or 14 years of age, but it meant I had a chance to be a professional footballer. My mate Clive Carter was invited to the trial as well. Clive played in the same team as me and he fancied his chances too, and it helped having someone I knew there. The days at Bristol were made up of training, across the road from the ground in Ashton Park. I used to get a real kick out of seeing some of the first-team players, like Len Bond or Chris Garland, coming and going and I used to wonder if that would be me in a few years.

My first game as a trialist was just outside Bristol at Keynsham Town's ground. It was trialists against trialists, with a few lads who were already signed thrown in. Dad had driven up for the game and it was great to see him. He told me just go and enjoy it. I intended to, even though I found myself playing left-back for some strange reason.

The game kicked off when, with five minutes gone, the ball came to me and I did a step-over to beat a player then passed the ball back to the 'keeper. The city coach stopped the game and asked where I usually played so I told him wide left. 'Well get out there then', he said. The game went well, with my team winning 2–0 and I set up one of the goals by putting a lovely cross into the box. I found that although I was a bit scrawny, I was a lot quicker than some of the lads and due to my experience playing against older players with Glastonbury.

The two weeks flew by and we had another series of games at Keynsham in the Cadbury Tournament, where I did well again. Heading home later with dad, we were both hopeful that I might get signed on schoolboy forms. I got back to normality pretty quick with school life and training with Glastonbury. Everybody was really pleased for me and they couldn't wait to hear how things went, but unfortunately despite my hopes, the phone did not ring and that letter marked 'Bristol City FC' never arrived on our doormat. Nothing happened for Clive either.

I was really disappointed, but dad being the brilliant parent he is, picked me up and told me that I'd get more chances. The same went for the lads at Glastonbury, who again told me I would make the grade. I never forgot the rejection at City but I never let it affect my football and that was evident when I got my Glastonbury first team debut aged just 14, at home to Weston-super-Mare. Manager Roy Hillman told me I had been knocking on the door for a while but now he felt it was the right time for me. I also signed a contract worth £2 a week, which was a lot better than doing a paper round. I scored regularly for the reserves, getting around 10 goals for the season, which was fantastic considering my age, and again I found the step up to the first team okay.

With things going well, I also got picked for the county team which was a great honour, particularly as it was managed by former Bristol Rovers winger George Petherbridge. George was a great winger in a great Bristol Rovers team of the 1950s. He was a lovely man who gave me tremendous confidence and he had great faith in my ability to go all the way in football. So much so that he contacted Bristol Rovers to get me a trial game. I had no hesitation in going for it, as the experience at Bristol City had made me more determined than ever to try and get an apprenticeship at a club.

The trial was at Rovers' training ground at Hambrook and as always, dad took me up and I met coaches Bobby Campbell and Roy Dolling, who put me at ease immediately. After the experience of the City trial, I was more prepared as I knew what to expect. The game was full of trialists and it really was about showing what you could do, and I certainly did that in getting a goal. The ball had fallen nicely for me from a corner and I seized my opportunity and smashed it into the back of the net. Our group of trialists won 2–1 and as I came off, the coaches told me I had done well. Dad and I spoke with Bobby Campbell after the match and he asked me to come back and play in some competitive games for the youth team, to which I agreed. The drive home was fantastic and although dad kept my feet on the ground, I knew he was pleased and I began to think maybe this could be the start of something.

I was playing regularly for Glastonbury Town first team and that had a massive effect on my game. I was getting fitter and stronger and to be honest, my confidence was sky high. So when I went back to Rovers, I really felt like I could do myself justice. I felt at home at Bristol Rovers straight away. They had some great people there, which helped, particularly Gordon Bennett, who worked with us young lads. Gordon told me that I would be playing different games at different levels so they could look at me. The structure was basically schoolboys, youth team, A-team, reserves, then 'the holy grail', the first team. As I was 15, I would be switching between youth team and a team made up of mainly 16 to 18 year olds, but that did not bother me – in fact, I thought it was a good sign. It was such a friendly club; it was the sort of place that if you saw a first team player, even if you were a trialist, they would still speak to you and I never forgot that. They made everybody feel part of the club. There was a real family atmosphere at Rovers and they made a real impression on me.

I played in various games and one in particular stands out with the youth team – away at Torquay United in the FA Youth Cup. We had some great players in the team, like Billy Foreman, Andy Evans, Vaughan Jones, Martin Thomas and Tony Pulis. We won the game 2–1 and I scored a cracker by beating the last defender and rounding the keeper one-on-one. It was the type of goal that would become my trademark over the years. I played in lots of A-team games for the club and I scored my share of goals in a period of about 12 months, gaining good reports from the coaches but nothing was offered. Surely I was doing something right, as I was still getting asked to play for them. But then Gordon Bennett put me out of my misery and told me he just did not think I was good enough at that time, but they would still be monitoring me. I think although I had done well, I knew it was coming; but I was determined it would not stop me in my dream.

I was really down after Rovers had said no, but yet again one man was there to pick me up and that was dad. I must admit, at that time I did start to have doubts about my ability. After all, what was it they were looking for? I was quick, I scored goals in the trials and I had not let myself down, so was I really going to make it? This became more of a worry as I was almost ready to leave school and it didn't look like I was going to be signed by a professional club, which had been my dream. I even had an interview for Morlands who were the local sheepskin suppliers and one of the biggest employers in the area. I remember being sat in the office, waiting for my interview, and looking around at everyone working and not speaking or smiling, and I thought, 'sod this, I'm off'. When I got home I said to my mum, 'that's not for me mum', and then they phoned up as they thought I had gone missing, but mum told them my future was not going to be in sheepskin. The following summer I left school without the dream move of going to a football club, so I went to work with dad at the very exclusive Millfield School in Somerset as a groundsman. My God I had a suntan that summer; it was boiling hot and I would drive the tractor around the grounds cutting the football, rugby and cricket pitches. Working with dad was great and being outside was a bonus, as I don't think I was cut out to work in an office or one of the local factories, especially at that age. But even with that job I never stopped working on my game, and at lunchtimes and after work I would go for a run or take a ball and just shoot into some nets. And although I had disappointments, I never lost my hunger for the game – in fact, I think I wanted it more.

I was still playing for the county team, under George Petherbridge, and he never stopped telling me that Rovers had made a mistake, which really boosted my confidence. At Glastonbury, a bad run towards the end of the season had resulted in Roy Hillman leaving the club. I had a lot of respect for Roy as he had given me my start at the club but his replacement, former Cardiff City player Peter Thomas, proved to be an even bigger fan of my ability, and in my first season with Peter I scored 24 goals. This resulted in Peter pulling me aside after training and telling me he'd had a word with Cardiff City and they wanted to see me. As you can imagine, I was ecstatic and couldn't wait to give it a shot. Dad left the job at Millfield so I left with him as I couldn't drive and I got a job at Andersons supermarket in the centre of Glastonbury, as a shelf-filler with my sister Lorraine. I knew time may be running out for me and I had to give Cardiff a real go. I was nearly 18 years old and trying to earn a professional contract, as I was too old to have an apprenticeship, and that would be harder. So it was off to Ninian Park.

Cardiff City were managed by Jimmy Andrews and at the time were in Division Three, but to be honest I didn't care where they were, as all I wanted was to be a player. I would be there for a couple of days while I trained and then play in a reserve game against Leicester City at Ninian Park. Jimmy Andrews told me to just enjoy it, which I did. I wasn't nervous and I couldn't wait to show them what I could do. The training was mainly ball work and running and I really felt good, and the lads were great, which helped. Dad was there for the match and I remember it was a terrible pitch, after a torrential downpour just before kick-off. I played wide right and made a few runs and caused a few problems, which was my game. I could whip a ball in with both feet and I was really pleased after the match, as Cardiff had won 1–0.

One of the coaches spoke with me and dad and they said they were pleased and would be in touch, so I said my goodbyes to the players and off we went, back to Glastonbury. But in the end, I heard nothing from them. When I returned to work, I could really feel everyone's disappointment for me and it was the same at Glastonbury Town; I really did feel people wanted me to succeed and I was touched by that warmth they showed towards me.

I enjoyed my time in the supermarket and I threw myself into the job, rising to the dizzy heights of assistant shop manager – much to my sister Lorraine's delight as she thought I would show her some favouritism. To be honest, I didn't really have any more power than when I was filling the shelves but I did have that assistant manager name badge. I carried on scoring for Glastonbury and that pleased Peter and my dad, as they knew I'd had some hard knocks in the last couple of years. But with the passing of my 18th birthday, I thought it was not going to happen for me at a professional club. The county football was going well and we were travelling all over the South West, playing other counties, but I have to admit, the highlight was when we played the army at the same Aldershot stadium where mum and dad had met all those years before. Everybody came to see but I'm sure mum and dad really wanted to reminisce about those early days. You could see they were thrilled to go back, and they gave us all a running commentary on how they met, where they first got chatting, how the place had changed. But once the game kicked off, there was only one thing on dad's mind. We ran out 4–1 winners and I got two goals, to make it a perfect day for the Randall family.

Chapter Four

The Rovers Return

Even though I was experiencing the disappointment of not having clubs take a chance on me, being involved in the trial games had certainly made me a better player. I was fitter and also a bit more tactically aware after my short time with professional clubs, and it showed in my form for Glastonbury Town.

In fact, I was getting well known throughout the Western League and there was talk of other non-league clubs becoming interested in me, but I never let it distract me. Come to think of it, nothing really got in the way of my football; I was never into cars or women although that would change later on. I would go out with some mates, usually Norman Hurd and Andy Wills, into the centre of Glastonbury and visit the local pubs, or Brewster's, which was the local disco. Trips further afield were also taken, mainly to the Red Lion in Somerton a couple of miles away, but for this we needed transport and that came in the shape of Norman's white Ford Anglia. The car was legendary as it could be opened and started up with any front door key. Needless to say, we would have hours of fun moving Norm's car after he had parked it, so that when he went to look for it he couldn't find it. On one occasion we went to a party in the car and on the way back, we had a couple of girls in the back. When suddenly we got a flat tyre. Unfortunately, I was so drunk I was slumped in the seat while they jacked the car up and changed the tyre with me still in it, none the wiser.

Norm has been another special person in my life. We met on the first day of school and sat together and we have been friends ever since – we even married sisters! Again Norm and Andy, who sadly died of an aneurism three years ago, were very supportive about my football career. Norm was also a good foot-baller and played for Glastonbury Town, but the limiting aspect of his game came when he tackled somebody and they went to the floor. He would help them up and say, 'sorry about that, are you okay?' We used to tear our hair out at him but he is a great bloke and I love him to bits.

On the pitch, things were going well and yet again, manager Pete Thomas never gave up on me. He used one of his many contacts in the game to give me another shot at trying to earn a contract at a professional club – and it couldn't have been any bigger club at the time. He contacted his mate, Ken Barnes, who happened to be the chief scout at Manchester City, about me and they invited me up for a two-week trial. When I think about it now, it just shows how the game has changed over the years, and not necessarily for the better. Can you imagine a top premiership team giving a trial to an 18-year-old player who was playing Western League football? It just wouldn't happen; they would think: if he hasn't been with a club by now then he can't be any good.

Manchester City were in the old First Division at the time and had just been pipped to the title by my beloved Liverpool; they had also come off the back of winning the League Cup and were managed by club legend Tony Book. When Pete told me, I couldn't believe that they would be interested but I couldn't wait to go and show them what I could do. Leading up to the trial, everybody was buzzing about the local lad going to one of Britain's biggest clubs, even if it was only for a trial. But I was quite keen to play it down, especially after my previous disappointments. I left with dad on the Monday morning; he booked some time off from work and as I would be in digs, he was staying at his sister's in Wigan. When we got to Maine Road, Ken Barnes showed us round and we met Tony Book. They told me to relax and enjoy the experience and I made sure I did. I sat on my bed back at the digs and thought, 'Paul, this could be it!'

There were a couple of other lads in the digs, which was close to the training ground, and off we went for the first day's training. I wasn't nervous, I just wanted to play. We trained on our own in the morning, then in the afternoon we trained with the first team. It was incredible for me – I was amongst players like Colin Bell, Brian Kidd, Joe Corrigan, Joe Royle, Mike Doyle, Asa Hartford and new signing Mike Channon. Everything went well and I did myself justice, although after a couple of days I wasn't England keeper Joe Corrigan's favourite person. One afternoon us 'stiffs', as we were known, would help Corrigan by taking shots at him. We would have a ball played to us by one of the coaches and we had to shoot then run round to the back of the line until it was our turn again. My first ball was played to me and I hit it on the volley and it went into the top corner and Corrigan never moved. My second shot went low to his left and again, he never moved. Then with the third shot, I curled it into the top corner again and with that, England international Corrigan walked off to get changed. I knew it had upset him and to their credit, the coaches did laugh, which I'm sure didn't help big Joe. Inside I was buzzing.

My trial game was against Stockport County at the training ground; Dad was there again as he had been in all the training sessions, trying not to look conspicuous by hiding behind a tree. I don't think he wanted to distract me. But I always saw him. The game went okay and we were drawing 1–1. I was playing well, then late in the second half a ball was played through and I left my marker for dead and struck a shot that went in off the post. I couldn't believe it, especially with Ken Barnes and Tony Book watching. The game ended 2–1 to us and I came off that field overjoyed. The training had gone well, and now I had got the winner in the trial game, but I tried not to get my hopes up, as I had scored in trial games before and after all this was Manchester City. Before I left, Ken Barnes invited me and dad into his office and Tony Book was sat there. They told me they thought I would become a player but whether it was at Man City was another thing. They said they were very interested in me and asked if I'd come back to play in some reserve games for them so they could have another look at me to be sure. I was overjoyed that they had not ruled me out and when somebody like Tony Book tells you that you can be a player, you feel 10 feet tall.

It was a long journey home but a very happy one. Even though I had nothing concrete, at least I knew where I was with them and I still had a chance. Word spread amongst the local press and the Western League that I had been to Man City and that they were interested in me. My form continued to improve and I found myself topping the Western League goal-scorers table midway through the season with 18 goals. In fact, under Pete Thomas I had scored 38 goals in 60 games!

The publicity also seemed to spark the interest of Bristol Rovers again. Colin Dobson, who was Rovers manager Don Megson's assistant, contacted Glaston-bury Town and asked if I would be available to play in a few reserve games for them to have another look at me. Obviously I was thrilled and I was happy to go, as I felt I was a much better player than when they had last seen me. I played in several games for them, notably against a very good QPR side – that included England international Gerry Francis – and Swindon Town, both at Rovers' old ground, Eastville. I played up front in both games and scored in the Swindon match. I was really pleased as the Rovers team was a strong one, with first team players Peter Aitken, Stuart Taylor, David Williams and Graham Day in the side – and I did not feel out of place.

Meanwhile Frome Town manager, Derrick Brain, had approached me and asked me if I would consider playing for them. He offered me £15 a game, which was quite a bit of money for a part-time footballer at the time. I was on about a fiver with Glastonbury and I thought long and hard about it – my main concern being that if nothing happened with Rovers and Man City, at least I could make a few quid. Also, no disrespect to Glastonbury, but the facilities at Frome were fantastic. So, with a genuine heavy heart, I left and went to Frome. Pete Thomas was great with me; he told me I would make it and I thanked him and the lads for everything they had done for me.

My first game for Frome was a pre-season friendly against Bath City, and it appeared my reputation went before me. Bath had a centre-half called Paul Grover, and before the game he came up to me and said; 'So you're the whizz kid everybody's talking about. Well you will have to get past me tonight, mate!' I did, and scored two goals but surprisingly I did not see Paul after the game. My second match for Frome was another friendly against Bristol Rovers, which suited them as they could have another look at me. Dad had spotted manager Don Megson up in the Frome stand so he said; 'Go on son, turn it on tonight.' I was really relaxed and I had a great game, scoring one after picking the ball up on the edge of the box and firing it into the top corner. Apparently Megson had left soon after that goal in the second half. I sat in the clubhouse with dad, and Colin Dobson came over to speak to us. 'What would you say if I offered you a contract right now, Paul?' Colin said. 'I would ask my dad', I replied. Dobson then told me that he and Don Megson were very impressed with me and Don would be contacting me at 2pm tomorrow.

I have never wanted the phone to ring so much in all my life. All my family were crowded around as 2pm approached. When it did, I picked it up and it was Don Megson. He told me that he would like to see me the following day at

Eastville with a view to signing for Bristol Rovers. The whole room went crazy. My mum and dad and sisters were jumping up and down screaming. It was a moment I will never forget. I'm so glad that the people who picked me up through the rejections were there at the moment a club offered me my dream; it was very emotional for all of us and that night I certainly didn't get much sleep. I lay on my bed thinking about this moment and how down I had felt after the rejections, knowing the next day I would be walking into a football club to sign a contract as a professional player.

My bosses at the supermarket gave me the day off as they were thrilled for me, and me and dad drove the 30 or so miles to Eastville stadium. As we drove we talked about the trials I'd had at various clubs and although Man City were still interested, I had always felt at home at Rovers. Even when they had rejected me the first time, I never forgot how much of a family club they were. Everything about them felt right.

Rovers were then in the Second Division and had sold their two strikers Alan Warboys and Bruce Bannister – 'Smash and Grab' as they had become known. So I knew they needed a goal scorer from somewhere. We arrived at Eastville and we were met by Don Megson. He sat us down in his office and said; 'There's a contract for you Paul, it's for one year. Hopefully, if you do well, we can extend it after the year.' I looked at it and it was for £55 a week with a signing-on fee of £250. To be honest, it was the same money as I was on in the supermarket but I would have played for nothing and I couldn't care less how long it was for, as at least I could say I was a professional player. I signed the contract, then I went out onto the pitch with Megson and had some photos taken for the local paper as well as an interview with Radio Bristol. They asked Megson why Rovers had signed me and he said 'to get goals', which gave me a big lift in confidence.

We were due to have a family holiday in Weymouth the following week and Megson told me to go for a couple of days and enjoy myself but be back for pre-season at the end of the week. I thanked him, then dad and I left. As we stood outside the ground, Dad gave me a massive hug and said; 'son, you did it'. To which I replied; 'no dad, we did it.'

The following day, I went to Andersons and gave them the news that I was handing in my notice. They were really pleased for me although they did say my job would still be there if it didn't go well, which was lovely of them. But I'd had my fill of stacking shelves. I also got in touch with George Petherbridge, who was equally thrilled and kept saying; 'I told you so'. Rovers sorted out a deal with Frome Town and gave them £1,000, which wasn't a bad return as I had only played two games for them. Glastonbury Town also received £1,000 as well as a pre-season friendly, which I thought was only fair. Then I had to make the phone call to Ken Barnes at Manchester City. Ken was great and he understood that here was a contract in front of me. He wished me well and he told me to give it my all, and that was one thing I was determined to do.

Chapter Five

The Arrival of Punky

Walking into Eastville Stadium as a professional footballer was the realisation of a dream. I walked in that first day and was met by first team coach Bobby Campbell. Bobby was a familiar face as he'd been the youth team coach when I had played a few games for Rovers when I was younger and he really put me at ease. All the lads were great; I knew some like Tony Pulis, Martin Thomas, Peter Aitkin and Phil Bater from my trials at the club but my overwhelming feeling was that they were a tight-knit bunch and they made me feel welcome. The most vocal was defender Graham Day. Graham was a Bristol lad who had come up from the club's youth system. He was a big central-defender who took no prisoners but he could play as well. He was also one of the funniest men I have ever met and it wasn't long before he took the piss out of me, mainly due to the fact that I had my kit in a Glastonbury Town bag. One of Graham's gems was when Rovers were playing Spurs at White Hart Lane later in the season. They were getting beat 9–0 and when the ball came out of the Rovers half, Dayo shouted at the top of his voice, 'CHARGE!' which had the rest of the team in fits of laughter, and some of the Spurs lads too. Dayo is also rumoured in that match to have told Bobby Gould; 'fuck off back up front Bob or it will be 10–0 with you in defence.' So with characters like that around, I felt really at home.

Don Megson, the manager, arrived and we set off for training at the park across the road from the stadium, which involved negotiating our way through the kennels where the greyhounds were kept. Eastville, at the time, still had dog racing so there I was, hopping from one leg to another to avoid the dog shit – not exactly a glamorous start to my career but I did not care. The session consisted of running and ball work. I really enjoyed it and I did not feel out of place amongst the lads, many of whom had come up through the ranks. I always looked upon my non-league career as my apprenticeship and I reckon it really put me in good stead for the rigours of league football. When the session ended, Megson told us that some of us would be playing in a pre-season friendly the following night at Trowbridge Town, and I was one of them. I couldn't wait to get started.

I was staying with another young footballer, Billy Foreman, in digs, with Bill and Ivy Parsons, whose son Lindsay was an ex-Rovers player but was then playing at Torquay United. The house was in Vassal Road, Bristol, and they really looked after us. Ivy would do all my washing and press my shirts, and she really became a second mother to Billy and me. Her husband Bill was a wonderful bloke and he would always ask about training and how we were getting on. And although I missed my family, I could not have wished to stay with better people.

The game at Trowbridge turned out to be a major factor in me getting my debut. We won 6–0; I scored four goals and it was a night where everything I tried came off. Dad was there and I spoke to him after. He reckoned, after my performance, that I would get to play in the first game of the season the following Saturday against Cardiff City at Ninian Park. I knew I had a chance, as striker Wayne Powell was injured, but I wasn't too sure until Megson told me on the Friday afternoon that I was in the side. He also told the local press that morning and arranged for them to come to the ground to interview me and take some pictures. I really felt like a star and just told the journalists that I couldn't wait to make my debut. After all the hype of the press, I phoned dad and he got all the family together to make the trip to see my first professional game.

The 1977–78 season was certainly one of transition for Bristol Rovers. At the end of the previous season they had lost Tote End heroes Alan Warboys and Bruce Bannister – otherwise known as 'Smash and Grab' – after they had both been transferred, and the fans were desperate for a new Terrace hero. In my wildest dreams I never thought it would be me. We opened our campaign in Division Two with the Severnside derby against welsh neighbours Cardiff City. I remember getting on the coach at Eastville and a lot of the experienced pros were playing cards at the back of the coach. I was just looking out of the window, thinking of the match, when I found myself singing along to a song by The Clash – one of the punk bands at the time – that was playing on the coach radio. Suddenly someone shouted; 'Oi, look at punky over there!' The nickname has stuck ever since. I am not certain who it was that gave me that nickname but it was a toss-up between Peter Aitken and Phil Bater – but even now when they see me they won't own up to it.

Peter and Phil were great lads; both had been spotted due to Rovers' superb scouting system in Wales and they had progressed through the club's youth system to become great players. When we arrived at Ninian Park, I went into the away dressing room and there, lying on my seat, were a dozen or so brown envelopes. I thought they were bills but they were telegrams from well wishers (people like my old supermarket workmates) a good luck card from the Western League, and messages from Glastonbury Town and my relatives, all wishing me luck. It was a wonderful thing to have before my first game. Don Megson gave the team talk and told me to go out and enjoy the game. Then the bell rang and out we went into a hostile derby in front of 7,000 fans. As I ran out, I gave a wave to the Rovers fans and I saw my family up in the stand: mum, dad and my three sisters. It was a great feeling. All the memories of my trial game for Cardiff City against Leicester came flooding back and I thought, well, I had a good game last time I was here, maybe I could do it again.

The first half was a typical derby match, very cagey with both teams creating few chances. I enjoyed it and we went into half time 0-0. Don gave us a few words and told us we would get our chances, and that I would definitely get the opportunity if I continued as I was going. Then on 48 minutes, our midfielder, David Williams, struck a shot that the Cardiff keeper could only push into my path and I stuck it away – off my shin to be honest. Although the ball seemed to take an eternity to cross the line, it did and I had scored my first career goal. I ran to the Rovers fans and to see the delight on their faces is something I will never forget. When the rest of the lads caught up with me they screamed, 'well done Punky!' but I will always remember our midfielder, Welsh international Frankie Prince, looked me in the eye and said: 'take your time going back to the halfway line son, and take it all in – this is a special moment.' I felt fantastic. If I never did anything else in football, that moment would have been worth all the heartache I had endured.

We held onto our lead until the 67th minute when Cardiff pulled one back, but the game ended 1–1 and I could not have asked for a better debut even though we drew. Back in the changing rooms, the lads congratulated me but Don was not happy that we had let a lead slip and he told us we would have to put it right in our home game the coming Tuesday night. After I got changed I was interviewed by the local press and I couldn't wait to read the account of my goal. The headline the following morning read *'Kid Randall Is The Supermarket Bargain Buy'*, which was fantastic for me and my family but the lads at Rovers never let it go to my head.

Our first home game of the season was against Notts County the following Tuesday, under floodlights at Eastville. There is always something magical about night games and I was really up for the match, especially when I could hear our fans in the Tote End singing my name just before kick off. The first half was goalless and I was tightly marked by Sammy Chapman who was an experienced old pro but I knew I had him beat for pace and in the second half I got my chance. At 47 minutes, David Williams put us ahead then on the hour, a cracking ball was played over the top and I left Sammy Chapman for dead. With only the keeper to beat, I put us 2–0 up and ran to the Tote End to take in their applause. That type of goal became my trademark over the years. After the Saturday result we would have expected to shut up shop, but yet again we threw away a lead and drew 2–2. Needless to say, Don was not happy; calling us unprofessional in the dressing room afterwards, but yet again the press forgave our failings and concentrated on Randall getting another goal. After the game I met up with my family in the players' bar and I also met ex-Bristol City and Liverpool player Peter Spiring, who came to see me and whose dad had got me the trial at Bristol City. He told me to keep learning and working hard and he reckoned I could go further based on the evening's display.

I remember getting back to Ivy and Bill's house and going straight to bed, but I couldn't sleep as I was still excited and replayed my goal over and over in my head. I think I finally dropped off about 2am. Our next game was a 0–0 draw at home to Fulham. After the game I felt a bit of tightness in my hamstring, so I spoke with the manager about it and he told me it was a blessing, as he wanted to rest me anyway. I remember feeling dejected but he knew what he was doing, although the team went down 3–1 to Blackpool in my absence.

I returned to the side in a 2–1 defeat against Luton Town and also a 2–1 defeat against Leyton Orient although I did get both our goals in each game.

It was a strange time for me; I had played seven games for the club and scored four goals but I had yet to be in a winning team. Then Don told me he was resting me again for the home game with Mansfield. I was not happy as I only had a year's contract and I wanted to play as much as I could to earn another, but I ended up in the reserves and a young lad called Wayne Powell took my place. Powell had showed great promise the season before, but my arrival on the scene had curtailed his chances and although we were great teammates, we both wanted that place in the side. Watching from the stands was not a great experience but I was pleased for the lads as they beat Mansfield 3–1 to register their first win of the season, and yes Wayne Powell scored one of the goals. And when the team remained unchanged for the next game against Burnley, I started to worry that my 15 minutes of fame were over.

The lads lost 3–1 at Burnley and Don Megson was starting to feel the pressure, especially as Bristol City at the time were doing well in Division One. I think Don felt he had to give the supporters a lift. I thought this might be my chance again, but on the eve of our home game with Blackburn Rovers he produced Rovers' new £10,000 signing from Wolves: Bobby Gould. Bobby had been there and done it all during a distinguished career with various clubs, and he certainly showed he had lost nothing of his goal-scoring prowess, getting a first half hat-trick on his debut as Rovers beat Blackburn 4–1. I remember thinking, hell, I'm never going to get in the side now. But Bobby was a great help to me. I learnt so much from him and he encouraged me and even told me to get a pension for when I finished football, which I did, so thanks for that Bob. I know that later when he became manager at the club, we did not always see eye-to-eye but in my time playing with him he was a top man.

Again I could not get back in the side as I was injured with a muscle strain that I had picked up in the reserves, so I couldn't go to the now-infamous match against Spurs at White Hart Lane. I had asked the club if I could attend a mate's wedding in Glastonbury which they agreed to, and I remember leaving the reception to go to the local takeaway as they had a TV on so I could see the result but the telly took ages to warm up. When I at last got to see the score it looked like 0–0, which I thought was a good result, and I couldn't hide my enthusiasm to the other customers, but as the TV picture got better and better, I could see it was 9–0 – for which everybody gave me so much stick I couldn't wait to get out. To be honest I'm glad I didn't play, as the game was on *Match of the Day* that night. Which only made it worse for the lads and supporters. I had experienced the highs, even if they were brief, and also the lows in my short Rovers career but I will always remember the next home game against Southampton. We drew 0–0 but I came to realise how brief a career in football can be, as my mate Andrew Evans, who was a great prospect at the club and a lovely lad with it, broke his ankle, and although he tried to come back, the injury effectively ended his career. It hit home to me that you have to take your chances and enjoy every moment, no matter how bad things may seem.

Don Megson recalled me for the next game at home to Millwall and I couldn't wait to play with Gouldy. We won 2–0 and it was great for us to get a victory for the fans.

But the win appeared to just paper over the cracks as we went to Sunderland and got hammered 5–0, then we lost away at Bolton 1–0 and on the Monday morning Don Megson told us after training that he was leaving the club to take the manager's job at Portland Timbers in the new American league. Don was a bit of a legend at Rovers; he had played for the club in the late sixties and had been the manager for five years. In that time he had won the Watney Cup and had got the club promotion but it had all started going wrong for him as we found ourselves struggling at the wrong end of the table. He came over to me the day he left and wished me all the best; I will always be grateful to him for giving me my chance. Rumours were flying about amongst the players as to who was going to get the manager's job, and I was worried in case whoever it was did not fancy me as a player – but then that's what happens all over the country when a manager leaves, so I don't think I was the only one in the Rovers dressing room to worry. But we did not have to wait long as Bobby Campbell was installed as the boss and Gouldy became player/coach. It was a great decision by the board from the players' point of view, as there was less upheaval and Bobby Campbell deserved it.

He had been at the club since 1961 and he was an old-school boss, a tough old Scot who I enjoyed playing for – and he knew the game inside and out. In Campbell's first game as boss, a 1–1 draw with Sheffield United, he put Wayne

Powell upfront to partner Gouldy instead of me, which I must admit unnerved me at the time – although I got on as substitute in Bobby's second game, a 1–1 draw at Hull City. I was starting to worry as I was not scoring and I'd only had three substitute appearances in the previous 13 games. I kept thinking about the fact that I only had a year to prove myself and maybe I had gone off the radar after such a great start, but I spoke to Bobby and he told me I was in his plans and to just be patient. Dad also told me that things would turn around and that maybe I was expecting too much. Then one day, Bobby came over to me after training and he placed 20 balls all across the six-yard box and just told me to hit them all into the empty net, just to get that feeling back – a training exercise which he often repeated and which really helped me. Then just after Christmas we played Crystal Palace at home and Bobby put me in the side. I was buzzing and couldn't wait to get going. I repaid his faith by scoring in a 3–0 win, which was our best performance of the season so far. That December, we also drew with Sunderland in the FA Cup at Roker Park and although they had murdered us on their turf earlier in the season, we looked like we had turned the corner as a team and we fancied our chances. I scored three goals in our next two matches and I was starting to get my confidence back as the goals started to fly in, and I have to say the 'Gas' fans never stopped cheering for me, even when I was not playing.

There were 27,000 fans at Roker Park, which created a really intimidating atmosphere, but I couldn't believe I was actually playing in the FA Cup as I had never got near any of the rounds in my Glastonbury days. Sunderland put us under the cosh from the start but Gouldy managed to grab a goal to put us 1–0 up. Unfortunately for me, I had got a dead leg and had to come off. I sat in the dressing room, icing my leg, pissed off to say the least, when I heard an almighty roar from the home fans and I thought, 'shit, they've scored', but then I heard the clip-clopping of boots coming towards the dressing room. The door flew open and it was Graham Day.

'Fucking ref sent me off,' he said.

'What for?' I asked.

'Fuck knows', he replied.

But we hung on with 10 men and found ourselves in the fourth round. We would find out on the Monday who we would face, but after that result we thought we could beat anyone.

I scored another two goals in our next two games, taking my tally to 10 goals in 15 appearances – three as sub. One of the goals was away at Fulham and the club chartered a train to take us and supporters up to the game. We were in our own compartment going up, but after the 1–1 draw we mixed with all the supporters and had a good drink with them all the way back to Bristol Temple Meads station. I just could not imagine that happening today as players are cocooned and kept away from supporters, which is a real shame.

Our fourth round opponents were to be Southampton, who had won the cup the previous year and had a really good side, but we felt we could beat them. The press got right behind the tie, both locally and nationally, and I was mentioned as Rovers' secret weapon, which was nice but did put added pressure on me, although I have to say that some of us did not have the perfect build-up to the game. We were a tight-knit bunch and a few of us – me, Peter Aitken, Graham Day and Phil Bater – would always go drinking in the Cross Hands pub which is in the Fishponds area of Bristol, close to where I was in digs. We knew the landlord well and would get him tickets for games, so on the Wednesday before the big Southampton match we went to the pub to give him some tickets. We asked for him and the barmaid said he was out the back. Minutes later she yelled out for us and we went running to the back lane, where we found him sat in his car with the engine running – a hosepipe leading into it. I smashed the car window and dragged him out as one of the other lads called for an ambulance, but it was too late – he was dead.

His suicide left us all in a state of shock, but I think it made us a bit more determined to win, if only for the landlord who was a big Rovers fan. On the day of the match, I woke up and as usual, Ivy made me some breakfast. I went to the bus stop at the end of the road and got on the bus for Eastville along with all the supporters decked out in their blue and white scarves. They all cheered and sang my name when they recognised me, which was fantastic for me. I made my way through the crowds to the players' entrance and, on entering the dressing room, went to my usual spot. I sorted out tickets for my family then got changed with all the lads. Then Bobby gave his team talk. He told us to give everything and not come back after the game with any regrets. I looked at the Southampton team sheet and they had some good players like

Alan Ball, Ted McDougall, Phil Bowyer and Nicky Holmes but I felt confident, especially with the Tote End on our side.

Running out was fantastic. Eastville was a lovely old ground that, over the years, had drawn some massive crowds. Its heyday was in the 1950s when Rovers were at their best, and to see it jam-packed is a memory I will always treasure. The game was a tight affair, with both sides going close. I got my first chance after a pass from Tony Pulis but the keeper saved well. Gouldy also went close and we were certainly not afraid of them. Then, a moment that changed my football career forever. On 44 minutes, Graham Day made a tackle in his own half, the ball flew up to me and I ran on to it instinctively and chipped the keeper with my right foot. Graham, to this day, says it was an inch-perfect pass but I still think it was a clearance. To see that ball hit the net was the stuff of dreams. I ran to the supporters and Eastville erupted like it had not in years. The lads jumped on me and we were all ecstatic. The half-time whistle blew and we went in on such a high. Throughout the whole half-time interval and Bobby Campbell's team talk, we could hear the supporters singing.

Second half, Southampton came at us more, but we were so strong in defence, combined with our midfield, which was slowly getting on top. Then, another ball from midfield, this time from Dave Staniforth, who was a big, six-foot lad from Chesterfield who had signed from Sheffield United. Dave put me through and I stuck it away to make it 2–0 to The Gas. Dave was tremendous to play with, he made loads of goals for me in my time at the club and he was a fountain of knowledge and experience for a young lad like me at that time.

As you can imagine, with that second goal the place went berserk, as did the lads. Minutes towards the end, Southampton fans spilled onto the pitch, trying to get the game stopped, but the ref was having none of it and carried on. On the final whistle there was bedlam, with supporters trying to get on the pitch, but we just managed to get off and then the celebration started. Although I had a got the goals, the whole team were magnificent that day, particularly Peter Aitken and Phil Bater. They never stopped running and tackling. Everyone one of the team was a star that day; it was a team I will never forget. Thomas; Aitken; Bater; Day; Taylor; Prince; Barry; Pulis; Gould; Staniforth. But it was Paul Randall that the local TV and press wanted to speak to, and I duly obliged, loving every minute of it.

And on Monday morning I was all over the papers as '*Supermarket Kid Sinks Saints*' and '*Bargain Boy Randall Does The Double*'. The papers were also full of First Division clubs interested in signing me; Leeds Utd, Aston Villa, Leicester City, QPR and strangely enough Man City, all of which were rumoured to be offering £100,000 plus, but I knew it was just paper talk. Bobby Campbell came out in the press to say he wouldn't accept anything less than £200,000 for me.

We all huddled round the radio at the training ground the Monday morning, listening to the draw for the next round, and up popped Bristol Rovers against Ipswich Town. We were thrilled; another First Division side at home. We felt we could beat anyone. Leading up to the Ipswich game, we drew 1–1 with Luton Town and beat Leyton Orient 2–1, with yours truly getting the winner. I was supremely confident that we could cause an upset. The press were getting their money's worth from me as I posed for photo after photo as the game drew nearer. I even went down to Anderson's supermarket in Glastonbury to pose with obligatory white hat and overalls. Stood by the meat slicer, I loved the attention and I think the Rovers fans loved the fact that they saw me as a normal bloke who seemed to have walked out of the terraces and onto the pitch. That's how the press saw it anyway.

Another packed house at a very snowy Eastville saw us go 1–0 down early on, but we got level in the second-half through David Williams, then minutes later Williams got his second to put us 2–1 up. The conditions were atrocious and in hindsight, the game should not have been played. It was difficult for us on the pitch as well as the supporters on the terraces. But through all this, we looked like we were heading for the sixth round when Gouldy put us 3–1 up, only for the linesman to flag for offside. It was a real blow as the goal looked like it should have been given. As we were getting over the decision, a lack of concentration on our part allowed our First Division visitors to pull the game back to 2–2, which sent the game to a replay at Portman Road.

We were despondent at the end as it seemed we had missed our chance. We lost the replay 3–0, ending our dream of a Wembley final, but Ipswich went on to win the cup that year so at least we were knocked out by the eventual winners – but it was cold comfort. So it was back to the league, and things were still worrying for us as we were at the bottom end of the table. I carried on scoring even though the side was struggling. The season was to end for us at Hull City in a real pressure game for both clubs. We needed to draw or win to stay up and Hull needed to win to stay up. It was a tense affair and I really did not want to be relegated in my first season with Rovers, but we got the win and I got the goal. I think it was one of the most important goals I ever scored for Rovers as it kept them up. The most ironic thing was that former Rovers legends, Alan Warboys and Bruce Bannister, were playing for Hull that day. We finished the season in 18th – one point from safety – as Blackpool, Mansfield and Hull City went down. I finished the season with 22 goals in 28 games (three as sub) and in what was really my first season, it was remarkable. It had been a wonderful first season as a professional, and in that time I had endured almost every emotion. I had scored, been injured, seen my manager resign and a new boss come to the club, I had been dropped and hit a barren run in front of the net, but had learnt some great lessons from some wonderful people. Now it was crunch time. Had I done enough to earn a contract?

I had to see Bobby Campbell in his office about my contract and before I went in Bobby Gould said: 'ask for as much as you can, son'. I went in and Bobby just came out and offered me another year's contract and £100 a week, which was double my wages, so as far as I was concerned, that was what I wanted. Now I felt like a real player, I was raring to go for what next season had in store. Surely it couldn't get any better?

Chapter Six

From Pirate to Potter

With the season ended, I left Mr and Mrs Parsons and headed back to Glastonbury. There was no training programme or diet plan given to me by Rovers, like the players get today. The backroom staff would make sure you lost any extra weight pre-season. Fortunately for me, I was skinny as a rake back then, but it never stopped me training all through the summer. I even went and worked for my mate Firenzo who was a builder. I was mixing cement and digging foundations; it was hard but it kept my feet firmly on the ground. I trained with the Glastonbury lads and though I felt I had improved as a player due to my time at Rovers, it was like I had never been away; except the whole town treated me like the local celebrity. I was inundated with offers to open fetes. Also, I got to open Bob Anderson, my old boss's brand new supermarket, which the local press had a field day with – more photos for their archive, of me with the white hat and overalls on. But I must admit, I loved it and always had a lot of time for the press people.

I would also get young lads waiting for autographs outside mum and dad's house, through the summer. I would be outside signing things for them and it was a dream for me, as I used to think not that long ago I was like them. They would tell me they were now Rovers fans, and how they wanted to be footballers. I always encouraged them to do their best and never give up on their dream.

When Rovers were ready to start pre-season they sent me a letter with a start date, so I contacted the Parsons and went back to Bristol. Billy Foreman, who I shared digs with in my first year, had been released. I was sad about that as Billy was a good lad, but my sympathy did not last long as Ivy told me I could have his room, which was twice the size of mine. 'Great, what a start to the new season', I thought.

Walking into the dressing room that first day was brilliant; I felt a bit more established and it was certainly easier than the previous year when I was the new boy. Things had changed a bit; striker Wayne Powell had left for Hereford United and Bobby had brought through some of the youngsters from the youth team, like striker Steve White, defender Vaughan Jones, and a lad called Gary Mabbutt who would go on to have a glittering career at Rovers, Spurs and for England. Bobby also had signed a lad from Walsall called Miah Dennehy for £20,000. Miah was a winger who had also played for Nottingham Forest. He was an Eire international who was a breath of fresh air in the dressing room. He had a thick Irish accent and we couldn't understand him half the time. He wasn't the brightest when it came to set plays; he never ever got to grips with our tactics for corners. We used a system where the corner taker (which would be Miah) would give hand signals to the rest of us; one hand in the air meant near post, two hands in the air meant far post, and touch the flag meant it was a short corner. He never got to grips with it. In fact, we got so frustrated by him we were going to write them on each corner flag, but he could play and was great company. He was also obsessed with the Nolan sisters, who at that time were a massive Irish all-girl group who had a massive hit with '*I'm In The Mood For Dancing*'. Miah claimed he knew them personally and for that we took the mick out of him all the time, but he never stopped telling us how close he was to them.

For pre-season we trained across the road in Eastville Park or sometimes we would go to Weston-super-Mare and run up and down the beach. Then for the ball work, it would be at the training ground at Hambrook. As I had kept myself fit all summer, all that running wasn't a problem and the whole squad were up and ready for the new season. Before the start of the season, the clubs were entered into The Anglo Scottish Cup, which was a competition between English, Welsh and Scottish teams.

Our group was Bristol City, Cardiff City and Fulham. The competition was a disaster for us; we started with a 1–0 win at home to Cardiff. I scored, after a clearance from Stuart Taylor in defence allowed me to run onto it, and I smashed the ball into the net. It was great to get scoring again and Cardiff were turning out to be a lucky side for me. We then got hammered 6–1 by rivals Bristol City; it was hard to take, especially as we went 1–0 up after youngster

Gary Clarke flicked home my header. Then Peter Aitken was sent off after a skirmish with Bristol City's new full back Terry Cooper and as a team, we just collapsed. I can tell you now; the dressing room was like a morgue after, as we really felt for the fans. Even though it was a pre-season tournament, it was still a local derby, and that kind of defeat was a real embarrassment. We were eventually knocked out after losing our final game 2–1 away at Fulham. David Williams got our goal from a penalty. I was substituted after having a nightmare game. We all re-grouped back at the training ground and vowed we would put things right for the forthcoming first game of the season at home to Fulham.

We did, running out 3–1 winners in front of 6,000 Gas Heads at Eastville, with me Gouldy and Mike Barry getting the goals. The joy did not last long as we lost our next two away games 3–1 at Oldham and 3–0 at Charlton, and the mood in the dressing room got worse as Bobby Gould announced that he was leaving to go to Hereford United. I had a lot of time for Bobby; he looked after me in my first season and made a point of coming to see me and wishing me all the best for the future. Little did I know that our paths would cross again.

Our first game without Gouldy was home to Cardiff City. I fancied my chances and that proved right as we won 4–2 through an own goal one from me and two from Dave Staniforth. Dave's goal gave me as much pleasure as my goal, as he was a real unsung hero who made loads of goals for me. After another home win the following week against Luton Town, with goals from me and Stanny, things seemed to have turned the corner, but we just could not win away, as defeat at West Ham followed. I had certainly started where I left off the following season, getting another goal in a 2–1 home win against Wrexham and taking my tally to four goals in seven league games. Yet again, the papers were full of stories of clubs who wanted to sign me. Sure, I was flattered, but I was happy at Eastville.

The next home game against Blackburn Rovers would turn out to be a game I will never forget for many reasons. It was a beautiful, sunny afternoon at Eastville. Mum and dad had come up for the game so I decided to go home with them after the match, which I did now and then.

Blackburn were struggling in the league at the time and Bobby brought in Gary Clarke for his league debut up front with me. Five minutes in and youngster Clarke whipped a ball in; Stanny flicked it on for me and I put it away. They equalised on 11 minutes but David Williams put us 2–1 up on 30 minutes, and just before half-time I got my second goal after a ball from Stanny allowed me to get in front of the defender and fire it home – making it 3–1 at half-time. I got my first career hat-trick in the second half after a Peter Aitken pass sat nicely enough for me to put it home. Blackburn must have been sick of hat-tricks, as Gouldy had got one the last time they visited us. The win put us in fifth place in the league, behind West Ham, Fulham, Stoke City and leaders Crystal Palace. We really started to believe we could do something this season.

I did not stay long in the players' bar so I jumped in the car with mum and dad and we set off home. On the way out of Bristol, dad stopped for a sports paper in the Totterdown area of the city. As I sat in the car waiting for him, the announcer on the car radio said that the young man who had been killed in the car accident on Friday evening had been named as Clive Carter from Glastonbury. Clive just happened to be one of my best mates; he had been with me when we trialled together at Bristol City all those years ago. I just went numb. Dad got back to the car and he could see on my face that I had found out what they had known since Friday. Apparently they did not want to tell me so as I could concentrate on the match. I don't remember crying, just looking down at this ball that everybody had signed. I still have it today; I think of it as a reminder of a great mate lost. Apparently Clive's car hit a tree as he went round a bend on his way home from a night out. The lads at the club were great and rallied round to support me. Miah made me laugh, saying that we should have a night out and he would bring the Nolans with him.

We failed to win away in our next game, going down 2–1 at Notts County, but it was nice for Steve White to get on the score sheet for us and I enjoyed playing up front with him. We produced another home-win, beating Leyton Orient 2–1. Again I failed to score and was starting to worry about it but the boys, and particularly Miah, had organised a night out after our away game at Leicester City as a way of letting our hair down and I thought it would do me good.

We drew at Filbert Street 0–0. In the dressing room afterwards, Miah was saying he was going to bring the Nolans on the night out and we were ripping into him, saying 'you lying git' and 'fuck off, you don't know the Nolans', and when we got back to Bristol he left us so we just thought he had bottled it so we went to our usual hangout – a club in the city centre called Platform One. It was about 11pm and we were all very well oiled. Suddenly, what appeared to be a white shining light focused on the main door. As it opened, there was Miah with two girls on each arm. We did a double take and realized it WAS the Nolans with him. He slowly walked into the club and the crowd parted as he approached the bar and ordered himself a Guinness. It was absolutely hysterical, he had known the girls for years and had contacted them as they were playing locally, which was why he wanted a night out after the Leicester game. It turned out to be a fabulous evening; I was star struck by them but they were so down-to-earth. The girls were fantastic company. That's all I'm saying about my night out with the Nolans, in case their lawyers are reading this (only joking).

That night out certainly did me the world of good as I got two goals in the next match – a win at home to Newcastle United. The away voodoo continued as we lost 3–0 at Fulham's Craven Cottage. Our next home game against Charlton Athletic was like a school football match as we drew 5–5. I managed to get the second hat-trick of my career in the game, with David Williams getting the other two goals. I scored in our next home game against Sheffield United. We beat them 2–1. I also had a good game against Stoke City in a 0–0 draw, but then I went on a barren run, not scoring in the next five games, although in that run we would notch up our first away win, beating Crystal Palace 1–0 thanks to a Steve white goal. I was really pleased as Dayo came up to me after and told me that my performance up front on my own was the best he had seen in years. A couple of days after the Palace game I was told to report to the Euro-Crest Hotel, Hambrook, which was next to our training ground. As I arrived, Bobby Campbell was there along with Stoke City manager Alan Durban. I asked Bob what it was all about and he said, 'we have sold you to Stoke City for £180,000.' Alan Durban shook my hand and said, 'right, are you ready to come up to the Victoria ground to sign?'

I was speechless, Stoke were a massive club and were on the verge of promotion to the First Division. There had been loads of transfer talk about me but it was done so quick I never had time to think about it. Looking back, Bobby was under pressure from the board to sell me, as they were skint; it appears they were going to take a gamble on playing Steve White as a replacement. I was in a daze – if I had said no, I would have found myself stuck in the reserves, as clubs held all the power then. It was so frustrating; we were going well in the league and they sold their top goal-scorer. I had scored 13 goals in 21 games so far that season. That's the great thing about this book – I can tell the supporters that I never wanted to leave and never left for money. It was a case of having no choice.

I had had such great memories at the club and had played with such great players who looked after me and helped me, but the worst thing about the move was the fact that I never got to say farewell to all those Rovers fans who had cheered me even when I wasn't scoring. If I had known I was going I would have enjoyed that goal against Sheffield United a bit more. So I gathered some belongings and left for Stoke with Alan Durban and a new chapter in my life.

Chapter Seven

Heading for the Big Time

Driving up to Stoke was surreal to say the least. My head was still in a daze – I kept thinking of all the players at Rovers I never got to say goodbye to. Alan Durban was brilliant. He was a top player in his day with Cardiff City, Derby County and Shrewsbury; and it was at Shrewsbury that he got his first manager's job, which had turned out to be a great success and consequently led him to be offered the Stoke City hot seat. I think he knew the transfer was all a bit of a rush but he kept telling me how he had bought me to get promotion and how next season I could be playing in Division One with all the big clubs. I must admit I was really excited when we pulled into the Victoria Ground and saw a group of supporters there to greet us. Stoke City is a massive club, as they have shown today, becoming one of the regulars in the Premier League – ironically under the guidance of my old teammate Tony Pulis until the end of the 2012–13 season. I thought about all those great players who had pulled on that red and white striped shirt over the years, like Matthews, Banks, Eastham, Shilton, Hudson, Greenhoff – the list is endless. It was hard to take in. I stepped out of the car and looked at this massive stadium – no disrespect to Rovers' ground Eastville, but this was something special. I walked into the ground and met all the backroom staff and coaches. Then it was time to sit down and talk contracts before I was unveiled to the waiting media.

We went straight to Durban's office where the contract was laid in front of me. When I think about it now, it's crazy as I genuinely had no idea how much Stoke were going to pay me. The most important thing was that Rovers got their £180,000. I seemed a bit of an afterthought. Anyway, Stoke were offering a three-year deal starting at £135 a week and rising to £165 in the second year, with a £9,000 signing-on fee paid in instalments of £2,777.66 each season, which would be taxed. I think I ended up with about £3,000 in total, out of the £9,000. I signed and became the West Country's most expensive footballer. It was also the most amount of money Alan Durban had ever spent on a footballer. So off we went to face the local and national press.

Alan Durban told them that I was here to score the goals to help them win promotion. He wanted me to link up with Brendan O'Callaghan who was a big, old-school centre-forward – much the same way that I had done at Rovers with Dave Staniforth. Brendan was a Yorkshire lad who arrived at Stoke from Bradford City a couple of years prior to me. He had become a bit of a hero at the club after scoring on his debut against Hull City with his first touch of the ball. Apparently, Stoke were waiting to take a corner when they brought Brendan on from the bench. They took the corner and he headed the ball home. It's a story he for one never grew tired of telling. I had the usual pictures taken for the morning paper, with me holding a Stoke City scarf. When it had all died down, Alan took me for a walk around the ground and at the back of one of the stands we bumped into Captain Dennis Smith, who was on crutches and sporting a massive black eye from a previous game. He was a massive man and he shook my hand and welcomed me to the club. 'I guess we're all set for promotion now boss', he said, to which Durban replied: 'you bet'. It gave me a massive boost of confidence.

The club put me in a hotel until I got settled. The next day, one of the coaches picked me up for training. I walked into what was a really experienced dressing room, with Dennis Smith, who, although on crutches, was just as vocal; Howard Kendall, who was a legend from his days in that wonderful 1960s Everton team; Mickey Doyle, who I had played against as one of the 'stiffs' in my trial at Manchester City; and Terry Conroy who, although nearing the end of his career, was still a fantastic player. Added to that, we had cockney Viv Busby who took the piss out of my accent right from the off, Big Brendan O'Callaghan and a smattering of youth, with lads coming through like Garth Crooks, Lee Chapman and Sammy Irving who all made me feel very welcome.

Training was a bit different to Rovers; there was still the usual running but the ball work was a lot more technical. At Rovers, the game plan was to rely on my speed to beat the last man. Here, I would be expected to hold the ball up and bring the midfield into play more. I was excited by this as I knew it would ultimately make me a better player. My first game was at the end of December, at home to Notts County. The weather had been terrible with snow, but the game went ahead. I could not wait to get started for my new club. My family came up to see me, which always gave me a lift. Stoke were around fourth in the league, so we needed to keep the push for promotion going. I had already scored 12 goals in this league this season for Bristol Rovers, so I knew I could get goals at this level. Again, no disrespect to Bristol Rovers but 22,000 fans were packed into the Victoria Ground and the whole of the Boothen End was swaying and singing – it was a fantastic atmosphere to play in. We did well, running out 2–0 winners, and although I had a few chances that went wide, I was happy with the debut. In fact, the local paper gave me a seven out of 10, which I knew wasn't that bad. More importantly, Alan Durban and the fans were pleased with me.

With the bad weather still about, we did not play our next game until 20 January, away at Brighton. We drew 1–1 and then had to wait until the second week of February until we got a point in a 0–0 draw at Luton. Even with the break in games, we were still training and I was still at the hotel being picked up, this time by Captain Dennis Smith who had returned from injury. He never stopped telling me that I should learn to drive – I think it was his way of telling me that he was only going to be my chauffeur for so long. So, I took his advice and had some lessons and passed first time, which was a real buzz as it meant I could pop back down to see mum and dad whenever I could, and I also did not have to listen to Dennis lecturing me again. So with my 'L plates' ripped up, I went and got myself a brand new gold-coloured Renault 18 car. Looking back, I don't think I could have got more '1970s footballer' if I had tried.

Staying at the hotel was pretty boring even though the married lads used to think it must be fantastic – staying at a hotel and being able to bring different women back all the time. I am not going to lie; I did have my moments with the opposite sex at that time. After all, a single footballer with a gold-coloured Renault 18 who lives in a hotel: it was always going to happen, wasn't it. But I must admit I enjoyed going back to Glastonbury now and then; being waited on by my mum and sisters. I also joined the Stoke City drinking team, which was basically me, Big Brendan, Sammy Irvine, Viv Busby and Geoff Scott. After training, it would be snooker hall and a couple of pints, then a lock-in at one of the pubs where the landlord was a Stoke fan. The drinking was the culture during the 70s; we had loads of time on our hands and the club never really kept tabs on you in terms of diet etc, like they do today. But even though sometimes we would get plastered, it was never before a match. We all had too much respect for our teammates and the fans to do that.

With the weather settling down towards the end of February, we gained another point away against promotion rivals Crystal Palace. Although I had not scored yet, I wasn't feeling any pressure as Brendan had put a couple away and we were working well together. The football we played was brilliant; it was always from the back we played, through the team. To see people like Howard Kendall at close hand, still running the midfield was a joy. We went into our fourth away game on the trot, against Burnley in third place. Although we had drawn the last three, we really needed to get back to winning ways.

It was a good atmosphere at Burnley's Turf Moor; the game was evenly poised when Big Brendan headed from a corner to put us 1–0 up. Then I picked the ball up about 30 yards from goal. I went past two Burnley defenders and the ball looked to be going out of play. With Brendan screaming for me to cross it, I managed to smash it between the keeper's legs from the tightest of angles and put us 2–0 up. It was a great feeling to get off the mark with my new club; I remember my old mate Frankie Prince – from my Rovers days – telling me to take my time going back and enjoy it, and I certainly did.

Garth Crooks got us a third as we went back to Stoke with a 3–0 win, still in second place in the league. The following week, we drew 1–1 at home to Preston then beat West Ham 2–0 at home. It's a game that I will always remember, not only because I set up the first goal for Mickey Doyle but also because I got the second. My first goal in front of the Stoke fans, it was a trademark rounding-the-'keeper goal. The game was on *Match of The Day* so I went back to Glastonbury to watch it with my family that night. I can still remember commentator John Motson saying, 'Randall's in here, Randall's in here', as I scored Stoke's second.

Another 0–0 draw at Sheffield United, followed by a 3–1 win at home to Leyton Orient meant we were still looking good for promotion. I was supremely confident of getting something against our next opponents, who happened to be Cardiff City – a club I had always scored against. I was proved right, as we won 3–1 at Ninian Park and I got my third goal for Stoke City – my 15th of the season. The spirit was good at the club as we came into the last few months of the campaign. We were feeling like we could do it but football has a nasty habit of biting you on the backside – we went down twice at home, losing 1–0 to our promotion rivals, Sunderland, and 2–1 to relegation-threatened Blackburn Rovers. Those defeats dropped us to fourth in the league. It was time we regrouped. This was when players like Smith, Kendall and Busby came into their own, drawing on all their experience to get us back on track. It paid off as we beat Fulham at home, 2–0, with me scoring our second. This win also got the fans back on side after two terrible defeats at home.

A draw against Leicester City, then a 4–1 win away at Charlton followed, with me getting one of the goals and taking my tally to five in fifteen for Stoke, so far for the season. Things were working well with me and Big Brendan up front. Alan Durban was very supportive, as were the supporters. After a 0–0 draw at home to Luton Town, which kept us third, with Palace first and Brighton second, we still had Sunderland breathing down our necks in fourth, so we could not afford to slip up now. The next game would be important to me in lots of ways.

Home to Bristol Rovers was a fixture I put in my diary the moment I signed for Stoke. I wondered what it would be like playing against a team so dear to me – now I would find out. My whole family came up and there was a lot in the Bristol press about me playing against the team that discovered me. When I left the club, they were fifth in the league but were now fighting relegation. I'm not saying it was down to me but it surely did not help – selling your top scorer just when you, as a club, could have pushed on and maybe got promotion. The Rovers fans were still not happy about me being sold and there had been hundreds of letters in the local press about it. There was a lot of ill feeling towards the board but thankfully, none against me.

I arrived at the game much like any other match, chatting and signing autographs for supporters as I made my way to the players' entrance. When the Rovers team had arrived, I went to see them and had a bit of a laugh with manager Bobby Campbell and a few of the old crew like Martin Thomas, Phil Bater and Peter Aitken. Kit man Ray Kendall called me outside. Outside was a brand new team bus, complete with tables, lampshades, and a toilet. Ray was the man who did everything for the lads and there was a little kitchen area so he could prepare the meals for the team.

'You paid for that', he laughed.

I couldn't believe it; the Stoke City coach never had a toilet, we just used a bin in the back row and if you wanted anything more than a piss the driver had to stop off somewhere.

'Fucking hell', I shouted. 'I hope there's some of that transfer fee left'.

We both laughed as we went back to the dressing rooms. The travelling Rovers fans gave me a great reception as I gave them a wave. I was determined that should I score, I was not going to celebrate it, and I think the Stoke fans would have understood why. We won the game 2–0, with goals from Viv Busby. As I left the field, my old captain, centre-half Stuart Taylor, told me – after facing me all game – that he thought I had become a much better player, which was a lovely thing for him to say.

The pressure was building on Stoke. We were in third spot with Sunderland right behind us, with only three games left to play. Off the field, I had moved into digs, which the club had found for me with a lovely couple called Mr and Mrs Dixon, who had a young son and an 18-year-old daughter who had been Miss Stoke-on-Trent – much to the delight of the rest of the Stoke lads. It's safe to say I enjoyed being in those digs; in fact, I don't think I had stayed in so much since I was a schoolboy. A 1–0 away to Wrexham, followed by a home draw with Newcastle, set everything up for the last day of the season. We were away at Notts County and Sunderland were at Wrexham – we were level on points so we just had to match Sunderland's result and we would be promoted with champions Crystal Palace and second place, Brighton. The crowd at Meadow Lane that day is something I will never forget – there were 22,000 in the crowd and I would say three-quarters were Stoke fans. It was a sea of red and white.

The game was a tense affair. Then, with 10 minutes left, news came that Sunderland were 2–1 up. I remember looking at the bench and seeing Alan Durban screaming for us to get forward, as we now needed a goal. With time ticking away, the crowd had gone silent. With two minutes remaining, I picked up the ball on the left wing, beat the full–back and crossed with every bit of strength I had left. I can then remember watching Paul Richardson knock it into the back of the county net to make it 1–0. The whistle blew and the place just erupted. We had done it; got promotion to the first division and pipped Sunderland by a point to finish the season in third. I found enough energy to run off the pitch with the other lads and the dressing room was madness; there were Champagne corks flying off in every direction, people were jumping in the bath (some of them were supporters who had got in to celebrate with us). We went back into the stand to take the applause of the travelling Stoke fans when we got back to The Potteries; we had a marvellous time.

The day after, there were a few sore heads at the civic reception to meet the Lord Mayor, but we all behaved ourselves. Then we flew off to Magaluf in Spain for a real party. I had never flown before and had never been to Spain, that's for sure. All I remember is burning like a crisp in the heat. The little drinking club we had going took things to a different level, with a drunken Big Brendan and Sammy Irving almost getting arrested after demanding that they be given keys to their rooms, only to discover they were in the wrong hotel.

As for me, well I enjoyed the Spanish nightlife and the female company – in fact I don't think I slept in my room more than twice in the week. Again, Alan Durban and the club were brilliant; they treated us as adults even if we did not deserve it at times. But they felt after a long, hard season we had earned the right to let our hair down. I was happy with my goal tally of 17 goals for the season, even though I had 12 of those at Rovers, and the thought of going to my beloved Liverpool to play, as well as Old Trafford, meant I couldn't wait for the new season to begin. As I sat by the pool with Brendan, beers in hands, dangling our feet in the cool water, I said to him: 'I don't think my football career could get any better, Brend'.

Chapter Eight

Hang on in There

After Magaluf, I went back to Glastonbury for a bit of peace and quiet. Everybody around the town was keen to speak to me about the new season ahead for Stoke City. They all wanted to know how I was getting on up there. I trained with some of the lads at Glastonbury and they gave me the usual stick about now being a First Division footballer. After a couple of weeks' rest I left and drove up to Stoke for pre-season. The squad had not really changed, although Howard Kendall had left to become Player Manager at Blackburn Rovers. He was a real loss, Howard; I got on with him well and I was sad to see him go, but you could tell he was destined to be a top manager – as he later showed at Everton. It's sad that he is not in football at the moment in some capacity, as his experience surely could be used. The squad had a new influx of younger lads including Lee Chapman; and Garth Crooks had become more established, along with a youngster called Adrian Heath from the youth team, and Geordie midfielder, Paul Bracewell. Other than that, it was more or less the same. We were a bit top-heavy when it came to forwards; with all these young lads, myself, Viv Busby and Big Brendan, we were all going to be fighting for places. We played a few pre-season games against local sides and everything went well; the excitement of being in the top division ran through the side. Our first game was to be home to Coventry City.

The day before the big match, Alan Durban sat us down and told us the side he'd picked. Jones, Evans, Scott, Irvine, Smith, Doyle, Busby, Heath, O'Callaghan, Crooks, Ursem and sub Richardson. I looked around and thought, 'did he say Randall?' And no, he did not say Randall. Durban came over to me and told me he wanted to play Big Brendan with Crooksy up front, with Viv and Adrian Heath wide. I was upset but I understood that he was the manager and that was his job to pick the team. The lads were brilliant; they knew I was upset but they all rallied round and took the piss out of something, which took my mind of it. So, as 23,000 screaming fans saw Stoke City mark their return to the big time, I found myself in front of 3,000 fans as the Stoke reserves played away at Sheffield Wednesday. It wasn't how I had imagined the season to start out for me.

The reserves got beat 3–0 and the first team won 3–2, with goals from Viv Busby and two from Garth Crooks. Durban was right in his team selection – after all, a win is a win. Again, I was not picked for the next two games – a 1–0 defeat against Nottingham Forest and a 3–1 win at home to Spurs. With a home League Cup game against second division Swansea City next up, I felt I might get my chance in the first team, but again I was left out as the lads drew 1–1. I was disappointed; I could score goals and I just wasn't getting my chance. It was like being 16 again, waiting for somebody to take a chance with me. What made it worse was that I was getting goals in the reserves but obviously Durban had set out his plans for the season. After training, he pulled me aside and told me I was in the side to play Ipswich away. I was really pleased. Durban was playing me wide right, and although it was not my preferred position I did not care. Viv Busby was moved to sub but he was really pleased for me. It was my first taste of Division One. You could tell the players were better and the game quicker, but we lost to a very good Ipswich team, 3–1. I did okay and was overjoyed when Alan Durban kept the same side for the second leg of the League Cup tie at Swansea City. We won 3–1 after extra time, with Crooksy getting two and yours truly getting the other. To score was fantastic; it rekindled my belief that I was worth a place in the side. All the backroom staff were pleased for me, especially my reserve team boss, Tony Lacy, who always believed I should be in the first team. Alan Durban was first to say well done when we got to the dressing room.

The club decided that we should stay over in a hotel after the game and travel back at 8am the next morning, so with that in mind, some the lads decided that it was a good excuse to see the nightlife of Swansea. That was the thing with the Stoke lads, although I was not in the side, I was still very much part of the team. Reserves and first teamers all trained together and went out socially together. I think if it had been any different, it might have added to the disappointment of not being in the side. So after a couple of pints in various pubs, we hit the nightclubs. It was nice to know that I still had not lost the old Randall magic. I came back to the hotel about 7.45am the following morning and just made the team coach.

After doing so well at Swansea, on and off the pitch, my confidence was sky high. Durban told me he was keeping the same side for the home visit of Everton. I phoned dad to tell him, and he made sure he was there with members of my family. So it became a real Randall day out, with people coming down from Merseyside to see the game. All I could ask for was a run in the side, and fair play to Durban, it seemed that was what he was doing. Another full house at the Victoria Ground saw us lose 3–2 –Dennis Smith and Brendan getting the goals. I had a few chances, which maybe I should have taken, but typical of the way things were going for me, I took a knock on my ankle, which flared up after the game and forced me to miss the next three – one of which was away at Bristol City. This match I had set my heart on playing in, especially as I knew I would have got a hostile reception with my connections with the blue side of Bristol. I travelled home to Glastonbury anyway that weekend to see the family. I knocked on my mum and dad's door and a strange woman opened it. She could see I was shocked. I asked her if Ken and June Randall were in. She told me they had moved to a house a couple of streets away. Yes that's right; mum had been up to her old tricks again and moved the family and had not even told me. When I found the right house, I gave her so much stick – in fact, I still wind her up about it today.

I missed Stoke's 2–1 home defeat to Crystal Palace and a 2–2 draw at home with Swindon Town in the League Cup, but I was brought back as sub for the away game with Manchester United. To play at Old Trafford is every footballers dream; even though I was sub, I was determined to take it all in. Everything about the place, from driving up and seeing it first-hand, to arriving at the dressing rooms and seeing your kit laid out, is something special. I felt like a kid and I just wanted to do myself justice. 52,000 saw Stoke get a real 'welcome to Division One' as United beat us 4–0. I got on for 20 minutes in place of Adrian Heath. I remember United's full-back, Arthur Albiston, hitting me with a tackle, and as I got up I thought, 'what the fuck was that?' That was one of the differences in the top division; when defenders tackled you, you felt it.

The defeat left Stoke in the bottom six. I had yet to be on the winning side in the league, which was something that was always at the back of my mind. It was one statistic I desperately wanted to get rid of. I kept my place in the side for the League Cup third round replay, away at Swindon Town, with Viv Busby moving to the bench. Durban put Lee Chapman up front with Crooksy, and me wide right. We lost 2–1. I was pleased for Lee as he got his first goal of the season, which I think was celebrated in various bars around Stoke. I got on really well with Lee; around this time we started to think about becoming flatmates. We rented a flat above a laundrette in Stoke for £10 a week. Things had become a bit awkward at Mr and Mrs Dixons; I was out with the lads most nights and coming home at all hours so I think they were a bit relieved when I left. As you can imagine, a nice clean house wasn't really a priority for two young, single footballers, and many a time Lee's lovely mum Jill would come round and collect our washing and make sure we had a Sunday dinner. I could probably write another book on what went on in that flat but I think I will leave it up to your imagination.

On the field, I found myself in and out of the side, playing only a handful of first-team games, either wide-right or as sub. Even though the lads made me feel part of the team, it was a bit soul-destroying getting goals in the reserves and it making no difference in helping me get a run in the side. Being in that situation, I suppose I should have banged on Alan Durban's office door, but it just wasn't my way. I was enjoying my time at Stoke, yet I wasn't in the team every week and when I was I was wide-right it just seemed as though Alan was as good as his word – he only bought me to get promotion. Nowadays I would have had an agent trying to engineer me a move away but football was different then; it was more in the power of the clubs. After getting a couple of goals in the reserves, Durban picked me as sub against Wolverhampton Wanderers at home. Although we suffered another 1–0 defeat, after the game Durban had commended me on my attitude through the last couple of weeks. I got my first taste of victory in a Stoke shirt after beating Bolton Wanderers 1–0 at the Victoria Ground. It was extra special as I crossed from the right for Big Brendan to head home the winner; it was just like the old days!

As December approached, we were beaten 3–1 away at Southampton then won 3–2 at home to West Brom, thanks to a Garth Crooks hat-trick. We then went to Crete for a mid-season break, where we were to play Greek first division side, Ophy FC. Alan Durban and Chairman Thomas Degg made sure we realised this was not an end of season tour; we had to treat this like a European tournament, and we had to be ambassadors for the city of Stoke. To the lads' credit, this is what we did but it was really funny looking back at that trip. We arrived and Durban had us out training, then he had us running outside our hotel; sprinting around roundabouts up and down the road. Christ knows what it must have looked like to the locals; they must have thought we were mad.

Then when it came to the match, we went to the stadium, which was a football pitch with maybe a bit of grass and a breezeblock wall all the way round. The changing rooms had no electric so we got changed in the dark. So out we run into the blistering heat and line up with our opponents. They are in all black, exactly like the ref, and it was a nightmare. I think I marked the ref twice when they had a corner. We won the game 1–0 due to a Brendan goal, and behaved ourselves without incident, which is more than I can say for the journey home. We got delayed and had to fly via Athens, Zurich and Heathrow, arriving home just hours before driving straight to Brighton to play them in the league. I am amazed to this day at how we did it and got a 0–0 draw.

After the point at Brighton, we lost 2–0 at home to Leeds United, which left us still in the bottom six. This was followed by another little milestone for me; an away game at Manchester City, the place that maybe I could have gone to if Rovers had not signed me.

A lot of the staff remembered me and it was a nice touch when they all said how glad they were that I had made it. It wasn't long before the Joe Corrigan story reared its head again and made everybody laugh, although I'm not sure Joe recognised me as we kicked off. We drew 1–1, with Alan Dodd getting our goal. We ended the year beaten 1–0 at Spurs, which left us fifth from bottom in the league. With the pressure mounting on Alan Durban from the fans, we thought the FA Cup third round game away at Burnley might do our confidence the world of good. I had great memories of the tournament, but we put in a terrible display and were knocked out 1–0. A further 1–0 defeat at home to Ipswich meant that changes were on the cards. Part of those changes was that I lost my place to young Jeff Cook and Brendan lost his to Lee Chapman. After my disappointment of losing my place, I was called to Alan Durban's office, where he told me that Blackburn Rovers' boss Howard Kendall wanted me to go on loan and he thought it would do me good.

It is a weird thing to get asked on loan as you're unhappy that it appears your own team don't want you, because why would they let you go, yet there is somebody who believes in your ability. Blackburn were flying high in Division Three; I knew I would get goals at that level. Howard called me and said he wanted to play me up front, not out on the wings. He thought that after an initial loan, we could see about a permanent move. I was ecstatic at the thought of somebody like Howard Kendall chasing me, then days later my good pal Sammy Irvine had a car accident. Thankfully, Sammy was okay but he would be out for a few weeks, so Durban cancelled the loan as I was needed for cover. I was gutted; I could see Alan's point but the thought of what might have been stuck in my mind. Howard's Blackburn were on the up and gained promotion that year. I often wondered what direction my career may have taken if I had joined Blackburn. I found myself back in the reserves but picked up a hamstring injury, which compounded my disappointment at not playing. After a three-month absence from the first team, I found myself named sub for the away trip to my beloved Liverpool. I must admit, I thought I had won the lottery; after all the disappointment, being involved in that one game against my boyhood team more than made up for it.

I was sub for the game and another Randall family day out was called for. Mum, dad, sisters, aunties and uncles all sat in the stand to see me hopefully grace that Anfield pitch. When we arrived I soaked up every bit of the place; if I got on then it would be incredible but just to sit in that dugout was enough. On the way out to the pitch I touched the 'This is Anfield' sign, and to hear the roar of The Kop was fantastic. As I sat there in the dugout, I thought about all those games I'd seen with my dad and uncles, and here I was on the pitch. As I looked at the other dugout, there was Bob Paisley, Ronnie Moran, Joe Fagan and a young lad recently signed from Chester City who had just made it to the fringes of the first team. Ian Rush; I wonder what happened to him?

We were a goal down and chasing the game, when Alan Durban looked at me and said; 'you're going on, Paul'. Lee Chapman came off and on I ran. Paul Randall, the lad from Glastonbury, was running on to play at Anfield. People today ask me what it's like to play at Anfield. If I'm truly honest, I can't remember. You see, those 20 minutes are an absolute blur. I was so in awe of the place; I can remember going round Alan Hansen and Phil Thompson and having a crack at the Kop end, but I also just felt like screaming 'I'M AT ANFIELD!' I felt like a kid. Come the final whistle, we had lost 1–0 but I never wanted to come off the pitch.

After Anfield, I pulled a muscle in training on the Monday and had to sit out the home game against Manchester City. I was ecstatic to get the nod in front of Lee Chapman away at Leeds United, but we were well-beaten 3–0. A substitute appearance in the home defeat against Southampton (2–1) would prove to be my last game of the season, having aggravated the pulled muscle I got after Anfield. When I look back, it was a very frustrating season in the top flight. I had made 34 league and cup appearances but only got two goals. I eased my disappointment by hanging onto the thought that I had played every game either wide right or wide left, which wasn't really my game. In the reserves I had played 22 games and scored eight goals. It really counted for nothing, as the first team was all that mattered. The team finished sixth from bottom, which, considering it was our first season in the top flight, was an excellent job by Alan Durban. 'Hang on in there, Paul,' I thought to myself, 'and give it a go next season. Surely it can't be as frustrating as this one.' Little did I know, it would prove not only frustrating but interesting as well.

Chapter Nine

Bring Him Home

As a new season arrived at Stoke City I was desperate for a change in my fortunes. After Stoke's transfer activity in the summer, I really thought the 1980–81 season would be mine. Garth Crooks, who had done so well up front the previous year, had been sold to Spurs for £650,000, and Viv Busby had left to go to America and play for Tulsa Roughnecks. The only other additions were defender Peter Hampton from Leeds United and a few lads from the youth team. Durban had also switched Brendan O'Callaghan to a centre-half, so that meant three forwards out of contention for the first-team spot.

Yet after a few pre-season games, I found myself facing Bury in the reserves whilst the first team opened their second season in the top flight away at Norwich City. Adrian Heath and Lee Chapman were preferred up front. I took the decision on the chin but I think in the back of my mind I couldn't help thinking that I couldn't possibly go another season without playing regularly. I felt that my career had started to slow up; although I always got a good reception from the fans around the ground, I was starting to be the forgotten man. Then, out of the blue, I got picked for the bench for our second home game of the season against Ipswich Town. It was great to be a part of a match day at the Victoria Ground, even if I was only sub. I was determined to give it my all and maybe get a first-team chance. It was such a strange feeling, I felt like I was on trial again trying to impress the manager and get him to give me a chance.

We drew 2–2, with Leon Ursem and Lee Chapman getting our goals. I got on for 15 minutes, replacing winger Paul Johnson. I put a few balls into the area but never got anything near to testing the 'keeper. Alan Durban was happy with the side and kept me as sub for the next game at home to Manchester City in the League Cup first round. I was happy just to be involved again. Another draw and another 10 minutes of football for me as we drew 1–1, with Chapman getting our goal. I came on and replaced another winger, this time Jeff Cook, but at least this time I did enough in those 10 minutes to get a place in the starting line-up in the next match away against Nottingham Forest. I was up front with Lee Chapman, and I was really confident that we could do something. That confidence was shattered as we were well beaten 5–0, and probably the only Stoke player to come out of the game with any credit was keeper Peter Fox – as if it wasn't for him, it could have been 10–0.

Durban made five changes for the replay at Man City and yes, you guessed it, one of them was me. Adrian Heath returned to partner Chapman up front but at least I got the place on the bench. I really was starting to get splinters in my arse from that bench. We lost the game 3–0 and I got on for 10 minutes, replacing Heath late on. Dad and the Stoke lads were really supportive, as I had not become a bad player overnight; they all helped me keep my chin up. Even though I was out of the side I was still very much part of the social side of things at Stoke. Especially as I had now moved in with Lee Chapman. Our new 'footballer's pad' became the venue for many a wild party. When I look back, I'm not surprised Lee now runs a few restaurants and nightclubs in London with his actress wife Leslie Ash; he definitely got the taste for a good time from those parties we threw.

I was happy being at Stoke but I was extremely frustrated at not being in Alan Durban's plans. Back in Bristol, the papers were full of stories regarding Paul Randall not being in the Stoke City side. It appeared Bristol City were poised to offer Stoke a swap deal, with centre-forward Tom Richie coming the other way to replace me, but nothing happened. I have to be honest; it did my confidence the world of good to think that maybe a club out there wanted me, even if it was the red side of Bristol.

After a run out in the reserves, Durban put me on the bench for the home game with Spurs. I got on for 20 minutes, playing wide right, and had a couple of chances but we went down 3–2. Yet again I was left out, for the following four games. It was during this period that Alan Durban called me into his office. He asked me if I would be prepared to go if a club came in for me. I replied; 'well, would you let me go?' and he said he would.

That was the first time Alan had made any remarks regarding me leaving the club. Obviously there was the Blackburn loan deal but that was the first indication that he was ready to sell me. Back in Bristol, a whole campaign had started with the Rovers fans calling for player manager Terry Cooper to go and get Paul Randall from Stoke City. It started to gain momentum and letters in the local paper appeared.

Bristol Evening Post – Dated September 15th 1979
Every encouragement possible should be given to Bristol Rovers to bring Paul Randall back to Eastville. As we demonstrated against Watford, Rovers do not have a goal scorer capable of turning half chances into goals the way Randall can. Support is dropping because there is no personality player with the charisma to fire the imagination but Randall proved in his time at Eastville he could do just that. Even now, nearly a year after his transfer, Randall's name is still running around the terraces. It must be clear to everyone that selling him was a mistake, but now we have a chance to put it right. The Rovers board should make every effort possible to bring about his return – THEN and only then will the crowds return and we can start a serious threat to promotion.

MARTYN RADNEDGE
141 ROBIN WAY, CHIPPING SODBURY, BRISTOL

Durban told me Bristol Rovers had approached Stoke but Rovers were trying to raise the £55,000 Stoke wanted for me, so at the moment nothing was doing. I thanked him for keeping me informed and I thought long and hard about the offer from Rovers. The more I thought about it, the more I wanted it to happen. I found myself back in the side against Birmingham City and playing wide right. I now had a bit of a skip about my step as it looked like there may be an offer from Rovers on the horizon. I played well in a 1–1 draw but again I was relegated to the bench for the visit of Liverpool a week later. It was always special for me to play Liverpool as it was for my family. My dad came to the game along with my uncle Barry. I just hoped I could get on.

A packed Victoria ground saw us losing 2–1 with 10 minutes left. I came on for centre-half Mickey Doyle, as we chased an equaliser. The first touch I had, I beat one player and put a cross over the bar. Then on the 90th minute, a ball was crossed into the box and Lee Chapman headed on for me to volley it home. It was my first goal of the season and to say I celebrated was an understatement. I think all the frustration of the previous months came out of me as I raced to the fans to show them I was still a good player. As for my dad and uncle, they had jumped up when Liverpool scored – being Liverpool supporters – and had been told to sit down by the Stoke fans they were sat amongst. Then they went berserk when I equalized, so the fans didn't know what team they were supporting in the end.

I was sub for the next game away at Sunderland, which we drew 0–0. After an injury to winger Jeff Cook, I found myself in the starting line-up against West Brom at the Hawthorns. Meanwhile, I knew the Bristol Rovers interest was still growing momentum. My mum and dad kept me informed with the papers back in Bristol. I still couldn't get the thought of a return to Eastville out of my mind.

Stoke drew 0–0 with West Brom and again I found myself out in the cold for the next few games. I certainly made the lads laugh in training. I would sing from the old Englebert Humperdinck song; *please release me, let me go*, which even Alan Durban and the coaching staff would laugh at. After a couple of goals for the reserves, I was recalled to the starting line-up away at Manchester United. I played a blinder at Old Trafford, scoring one goal as we drew 2–2, with Lee Chapman getting the other. It gave me such a lift; I had scored against two of the best teams in the league and I felt like I had reminded the Stoke fans that I was still about. Alan Durban sang my praises after the game and kept me in the side for the home games against Leicester City, a match we won 1–0, and Aston Villa, to whom we lost 1–0.

Back at the training ground, I was told that Bristol Rovers had made a bid for me and it had been accepted. I was to drive down to the hotel near the Rovers training ground to meet Terry Cooper and sign. I picked a few things up at the Stoke training ground, but the lads were training so I did not get a chance to speak to them. I jumped in the car and drove down to Bristol to meet Terry Cooper and Rovers chairman Graham Holmes. I arrived at 12.30

in the afternoon. Halfway through the meeting, the phone in the room went and I answered it and the hotel receptionist said, 'Mr Randall, I have a Mr Wimshurst on the line for you down here in reception.'

Ken Wimshurst was Bristol City manager Bob Houghton's assistant. He had tracked me down to the hotel and he obviously wanted to sign me. I told Terry and Graham that I had to pop downstairs. I spoke to Ken in the foyer of the hotel and he told me not to sign, as City wanted me. I told him that I had given Cooper my word and I would not go back on it. Returning to the room, I took hold of the contract and signed. It was a two-year deal on £180 a week. The decision not to sign for City is one that I'm so glad I made; they offered me more money and are a good club but I feel I would never have been accepted by their fans and I think it certainly would have tarnished my relationship with the Rovers fans. I know some players have crossed the City but it just wasn't for me. Terry had told me that the Rovers supporters had raised all of the £55,000 to get me. It was a wonderful feeling to know how much the fans wanted me to come back. I drove back to Stoke to say my goodbyes to all the staff and pick up my things from the ground.

When I look back at my time at Stoke City, I still feel a lot of affection for the club. They gave me the chance to play at the highest level and they certainly made me a better player. I played with some wonderful players and made some great friends at the club. Alan Durban was a good manager and a great coach; he was honest with me and as a player, that's all you can ask for. I know people think that my time at Stoke was a disaster, but after getting promotion I never really got a chance to play up front and forge a partnership with anyone apart from that first season with Brendan. I have nothing but good memories of my time at The Potteries.

Bristol Rovers were a very different team to the one I left. Terry Cooper was player-manager and the job was his first step into management. He was a bit of a legend, not only in his days for Leeds United but also for England. The club also had a new board, but Eastville Stadium was a shadow of its former self, as a fire had ripped through the south stand months before. On the pitch, Rovers found themselves at the bottom of the second division. In the dressing room, there were a few old faces like Tony Pulis, Phil Bater and Vaughan Jones, along with youngsters I knew like Gary Mabbutt, Phil Kite, and a superb winger called Mickey Barrett. I also inherited a young, promising lad from the youth team to clean my boots, called Ian Holloway. The club was as friendly as ever, despite the troubles it had been through since I left. As for the fans, well what can you say about people who gave their hard-earned cash to buy you from a club.

I remember going with directors Barry Bradshaw and Martin Flook to some offices in Bristol and seeing sack-loads of letters with kids' pocket money in and donations to the appeal to buy me back from Stoke. To see it was very humbling and even today I get people coming up to me to say, 'I gave money to that appeal, Paul'. Gas Heads are first class! I did the usual photo call and interviews with the local press before my first game, which just happened to be a derby against Bristol City. 'The Legend Returns' was how the local press ran the story, so there was a bit of pressure, but I couldn't wait to get going.

I moved in with my mum and dad. It was cramped with my sisters still living there, but it felt really good to be back, particularly after my time sharing with Lee, which certainly wasn't without incident. At least I knew I would get a good night's kip before training. The game against Bristol City is always a massive thing in Bristol; it's a huge derby clash and the fact that I had returned made it even more interesting for the area. Both clubs were struggling at the wrong end of the table. I got a fantastic reception from the Rovers fans as I ran out to our biggest gate of the season – over 10,000 screaming Bristolians.

Youngster Phil Kite was in goal for us and we had ex-City player Donnie Gillies at the back with Terry Cooper to add a bit of experience. I was up front with Bob Lee, who had signed from Sunderland. I also found myself up against my old teammate Peter Aitken who had crossed the city to join the red half. The game was a tense affair; I remember getting a few chances but towards the end of the match I was absolutely knackered. I took my shin pads off and played the last 10 minutes with my socks rolled down. I realised I was fit but not match fit, after all those times in and out of the side at Stoke City. The game ended 0–0, which really was no good to either of us.

We lost our next game 1–0 at Oldham. Again, I had a few chances but the fans were incredible. They were so glad that I had returned, I just wanted to repay them with a goal. In our next home game at Bolton I felt I had started to repay the faith they showed in me as I grabbed two goals in our 2–1 win.

The first goal was with almost my first touch of the ball; young Geraint Williams pushed a lovely pass through the Bolton defence for me to round the 'keeper and smash the ball home. It was an incredible feeling; like nothing I had experienced. I knew there were people in that crowd who had bought me so I just felt elated to get the goal for them. My second was a header from a Gary Mabbutt free kick. I injured my hamstring going for the ball; another result of not being truly match fit. I stayed on and played the last few minutes in pain. Nothing was going to get me off that pitch. The whistle blew and the crowd was fantastic; we had registered a much-needed home win.

The second division table did not make for good reading for Bristol football. Even though we had won, we still found ourselves seven points adrift at the bottom of the table with 15 points. Our nearest team was Bristol City on 22 points, so it really did not look good for us. My leg was okay and I played away at Newcastle United the following week. We got our first away point of the season at St James' Park. I also missed a sitter from six yards out which played on my mind on the way home. I could see Terry Cooper was under pressure, as we all were. I certainly felt that if we went down, it was down to me. I was brought in to be the saviour; to score the goals to keep the club up and that's probably why I analysed every miss at that time. The tactics were different to the last time I was at Rovers. I was used to playing with a big man like Dave Staniforth at Rovers or Brendan at Stoke City. Terry was struggling with partners up front with me. Bob Lee was not having the best of times upfront and we never really hit it off. I also partnered Gary Mabbutt in attack, but he was more of a midfield player and didn't have the big physical presence I thrived off. Shaun Penny was the same. Even though we could see we were going to have a fight to stay in the league, the Gas fans still stuck with us.

I got another goal in a 3–1 away win at Cambridge United; it was our first away win in 23 attempts. We had another blow as influential midfielder Stewart Barrowclough left for Barnsley. The season started to get away from us and I found goals hard to come by. Sadly we were relegated with four games still to go, along with Bristol City and Preston North End. The only bright spark in the season's end was that my boot cleaner, Ian Holloway, made his debut as substitute against Wrexham, coming on late in our 3–1 defeat. I was really pleased for him, even if I did tell him after the game that my boots were in a right state and could he sort them out. That's the thing with relegation, it runs right through a club and it's a terrible feeling having to carry the thought around that you let the fans down. I felt it deeply as I was supposed to save them with my goals. I had only got three in 15 games. I knew it would be a tough summer but at least the club had a crop of youngsters on the horizon, like Ian Holloway, who might do something the following season under Terry Cooper; providing, of course, that the board stuck with him.

Chapter Ten

Hello Bobby

Relegation is a dreadful thing to have on your mind through the summer. And ours into Division Three made it a tough summer for everyone connected with the club. I couldn't get out of my mind the thought that I had let the fans down. I couldn't wait for the season to start so I could put things right.

I kept myself busy during the summer by doing some building work with my mate Vicenzo. I would also go out for a few runs with some of the Glastonbury lads to keep fit, so I was raring to go for my first full season back at the club. Behind the scenes there was plenty of activity at boardroom level to keep the local press interested. New safety regulations had reduced the capacity at Eastville and that had led to some tightening of the purse strings. The Stevens family, who had been majority shareholders at the club, lost overall control to local businessmen Barry Bradshaw and Martin Flook, who had both been instrumental in getting me back to the club. They desperately wanted a new ground for Rovers. Martin even offered Bristol City £450,000 for their ground at Ashton Gate, as City were plummeting toward Division Four and in a real financial mess. But thank God, City said no, as I just don't think it would have worked for us to go to the red half of the city.

Terry Cooper was still in charge of the club, which I was pleased with as he had a tremendous amount of pressure on him after the relegation. Terry had made a few changes; Tony Pulis was moved to player coach, which I was not so pleased with as Tony was a fitness nut. In fact, you only have to look at him today to see that he looks as fit now as he did then. I knew that we would be in for a few cross-country runs in training.

Terry also brought in a big lad at centre-half from Swedish club Malmo, called Tim Parkin. Tim was from Cumbria and always used to wear dreadful checked lumberjack shirts that we would hide if we saw them lying around the dressing room. Tim was a real inspiration to us all. While he was at Rovers he and his wife lost their young son to leukaemia. The strength he showed at that time was something I never forgot; he really was a great lad. Brian Williams joined us from Swindon; again he was a great lad who played full-back. Our last acquisition was a raw, talented forward called Archie Stephens. Archie was a painter and decorator by trade, who had scored loads of goals in the Weston League with Melksham Town. He said he was 23 years old but apparently he was 27. Archie would be playing up front with me. I couldn't wait as I saw a bit of myself in him. We also had the great nucleus of youngsters in the side like Phil Kite, who was pushing Martin Thomas close for the number one shirt, Keith Curle, who was a lightning-quick lad, and Ian Holloway, to whom I had become some sort of agony uncle. He would ask my advice on his girlfriend problems; and though after my reputation in Stoke I did not feel I was the best person to give advice, I loved Ollie to bits. I knew he was a real talent. I also got myself a new roommate for away trips, in the shape of Mickey Barrett; this would mean that he had to make the tea and look after me when we played away. Errington Kelly, another quick forward, joined from Ledbury Town, but we lost Phil Bater, who had left for Newport County. Phil was a real loss as he was a good player; I was sad to see him go.

We toured Scotland for pre-season, playing Ayr United, Partick Thistle and Falkirk and winning all three games which filled us with confidence for the new season. I scored a few in the games and played up front with Errington as well as Archie. With Archie, the partnership really clicked which made me really excited, as I thought to myself; 'have I found another Staniforth or big Brendan here?'

We opened our campaign at home against Chester City in front of around 6,000 fans. I played up front with Gary Mabbutt, who I have to say was a great midfielder for us. But I never really saw Gary as a forward as obviously Terry Cooper did. Archie Stephens was left out of the side as we ground out a 2–2 draw with our own Mr Dependable, David Williams, and youngster Keith Curle getting the goals. After the game, Coops gave me a bit of stick regarding a few missed chances but I just took it on the chin. I was paired up front with Mabbs again for the away trip with Chesterfield, but another disappointing display saw us lose 2–0. Terry had a shift around for the next couple of games, which saw me moved to wide left and Mabbs paired with Archie upfront. I can't say I was happy but I replied with a couple of goals against Reading and Exeter City. The only sad thing was the goals were both away so I didn't get chance to celebrate with the Rovers fans at home. I was paired up front with Gary Mabbutt again for the next couple of matches, with no joy in front of goal. After a 1–0 defeat away at Southend United, Coops had a real go at me, saying I was not working hard enough in front of goal. I never retaliated as I thought, well, he's the boss, and I had a lot of respect for him for what he had done in the game. So again, I just took it. I was getting the brunt of his anger and it came to a head when he dropped me for the next game at home to Swindon. I was dumbstruck. We had played nine games and won four of them. I had scored two goals so I couldn't honestly see that we were struggling. I thought my game was fine. But I thought, 'oh well, I better get on with it.'

It hurt like hell to be dropped. I had been dropped at Stoke but Rovers were my club and I felt a real sense of letting the fans down. The result at home to Swindon was a real surprise. We were thumped 4–1 and the Rovers faithful were not happy at the end of the 90 minutes, booing the team and singing my name which was nice but put more pressure on Coops. The next morning I woke up to be greeted by my mum bringing me a cup of tea and telling me that she had just heard on the radio that Terry Cooper had been sacked. I couldn't believe it; I knew Terry was under pressure all through the last season but it appears the directors had thought it was time for change. I picked up defender Donnie Gillies, who lived by me, and we set off for training in Bristol. When we got to the Hambrook training ground, we were met by Terry picking up his belongings. He shook our hands and wished us all the best and told us to take care. That showed what a top bloke he was; even though he was hurting from the sacking he still wished all the lads the best. I will always be grateful to him for bringing me home to Rovers.

All the lads were stunned by the sacking but we had to prepare for a trip to Oxford United in the week. The Rovers board put Ron Gingell in charge for the game. Ron was the club's chief scout; he had been a full-back at Chelsea and Exeter City in his time and did not seem worried by the new job. He certainly got me on his side by picking me as sub. I was thrilled to be involved with the lads again. Ron had told me on the coach up that I would get on for the second half so I was buzzing. We went 1–0 down after a mistake by young keeper Phil Kite, but we just kept at them. Then in the second half, Ron sent me on for Mark Hughes and pushed Gary Mabbutt back to midfield, which left me and Archie up front. With a quarter of an hour to go, a lovely through ball allowed me to run onto it and smash home the equaliser. It was great to see that ball hit the net, especially for the fans who had travelled, as well as Ron Gingell, who it later turned out was the only ever Bristol Rovers manager to never lose a game. My dad was also there; he had taken the afternoon off work to come up. The game ended 1–1. I saw dad before I got on the coach and he told me he had met a lovely bloke in the car park who was going to be our next boss. Trust dad to find out before me. Apparently he was walking to his car when Bobby Gould came up to him. Bobby asked dad if I was okay, as I didn't look the same player as when he saw me last. Dad replied; 'well if you're not scoring as a striker, you're not in the team, Bob.' Then typically, dad asked Bobby if he had the job. To which Bobby said yes.

I kept the news to myself but I did tell Donnie Gillies who said; 'well that's me fucked then.' You see, Donnie and Bobby did not see eye to eye with each other from their days at Bristol City when they were teammates – and I use that term very loosely. Allegedly Bobby used to take a briefcase in to work with him when he was at Bristol City and Donnie may have put something in it that he should not have (I will leave it at that). A couple of days later, Bobby was installed as the new Bristol Rovers boss on a three-year contract. I was pleased with Bobby's appointment. He had been good to me when we played together and he was always willing to give advice. Bobby's first game in charge was at home to Huddersfield Town. 6,000 turned up to show their support. It was a thrilling encounter that saw us win 3–2 against the Yorkshire men; myself, Archie Stephens and big centre-half Aidan McCaffery getting the goals, which left us mid-table in the league. Bob was over the moon with the win. He kept telling us that we could really do something this season.

We lost our next game away 4–2 at Doncaster Rovers, with Archie and Mabbs getting the goals. I was still playing wide right but I was enjoying my football. As for training, Bobby decided that, following the defeat; maybe we needed a different type of warm up. He had seen a TV programme about the great

Brazilian side of the 70s and their training methods and decided we would do it the Brazilian way, which meant we would skip in twos with Bobby telling us to touch our heads, then our shoulders, then our knees as we ran along. Now this probably looked great on the Copacabana beach in Rio, but on a rainy day in Bristol it just looked ridiculous. We pissed ourselves laughing but Bob kept on shouting at us to continue. Another one of Bob's 'methods' was to have a chart on the wall of his office, with stars of different colours against our names. To this day, I still do not know what on earth they meant, but I do know that Donnie used to sneak into Bobby's office and move them about. It's no wonder Donnie left after a few months with Bobby as his boss.

In our next two games at home, we beat Newport County 2–0 and Gillingham 2–0. I had moved back to partner Archie up front. I got a goal in each game, which meant that I had got three goals in four matches for Bobby. We had a real team spirit at the club. Bobby's coaching on the training field was top drawer; he made training really enjoyable for us, even though we were skipping about like Brazilians. He was the first coach I had ever worked with who had told us about getting balls into the box with speed as they were difficult to defend against. You could tell he had been there and done it. Archie and myself were working well together. He was loving being a full-time pro but I do recall another one of Bobby's special ideas having a great effect on Archie. Bobby told us that we were going to give something back to the community. He decided after training that we were going to repaint Eastville. He bought us all the paint, dustsheets, rollers and brushes and we were stunned. I was painting the open end at the ground with Archie when he said, 'I don't fucking believe this. I became a footballer to get away from fucking painting.' We just fell about laughing. That was Bobby for you.

The young lads at the club were doing well, although Phil Kite had just lost his place to the more experienced Martin Thomas. Keith Curle was becoming a revelation with his speed and he was chipping in with a few goals. But Gary Mabbutt was really shining, both in midfield and up front. Gary was a great lad whose dad Ray had played for Rovers in the 1950s. While Gary was at Rovers, his older brother Kevin was making a name for himself at Bristol City – before a big-money move took him to Crystal Palace. Gary was a good lad but he was without doubt the worst dressed bloke I ever met. He also had the worst taste in music. The lads hated getting a lift from him, as he would play the *Mary Poppins* soundtrack in his car. Gary was a real talent and had overcome being a diabetic to become a footballer. It meant he had to give himself insulin every day with an injection but it never stopped him becoming a top player. As for my ex-bootboy Ollie, a combination of injuries and loss of form kept him out of the side. I kept his spirits up and told him to keep his chin up, and to be fair to him, he was still a laugh around the place – even though he was hurting from not playing. Winger Mickey Barrett was still playing out of his skin out on the wing; he was also doing a great job on away games making my tea whenever I wanted.

One away game that I remember from that season is Millwall at the old Den. Games at Millwall could be very intimidating as the crowds were right on top of you. The supporters had a fearsome reputation. In this game, we had drawn 0–0 and after the game I, along with Archie, gave kit man Ray Kendall a hand loading the big wicker cases that held the kit onto the coach. All of a sudden, a group of Millwall fans came towards us and in his best cockney voice, one of them said; 'we'll 'ave that mate.'

I said, 'what?'

'That fuckin' kit', they replied.

One of them punched me in the side of the head and I fell, dazed, against a wall. Suddenly, the police came running around the corner so the Millwall fans ran off. I have never been so pleased to see the boys in blue; it was a real bizarre situation and looking back, I was lucky I did not get a good kicking.

Towards the end of the year, I had a bit of a barren spell, going five games without scoring, but it was at times like this that Bobby really came in to his own – being an ex-striker. He would encourage me and work on my finishing. I was desperate to get back on the goal trail, especially with the big Bristol derby coming up just after Christmas. The Bristol derby is a fantastic occasion for the whole of the area. I don't think there is anything like a derby where you have two teams in the one city. As a player, you just want to do well for the fans so they can go to work on the Monday with a smile on their faces. This was our first meeting of the season. City was struggling at the bottom of the table, so we really fancied our chances, especially with a good crowd behind us. A crowd of 12,000 crammed into Eastville, and we won with a solitary

Aidan McCaffery goal, ensuring the bragging rights for the rest of the season. I picked up a knock, which meant I missed our next game away at Plymouth Argyle. I'm glad I did, as Bobby showed what a one-off he is. We were beaten 4–0 and Bobby was not at all happy, so, according to our kit man Ray Kendall, Bob got all the players on the coach and banned everyone from having one of Ray's microwave meals that he usually prepared for the team. Bobby wanted the players to be hungry and think about how they had let everybody down, which was okay for all the lads except for young Gary Mabbutt, who had to have food after a game on doctor's orders due to his diabetes. The lads ended up smuggling biscuits up to Gary. Bobby sat at the front of the coach, blissfully unaware that one of his players could have slipped into a coma. After my injury, I got back to finding the net in the following two games; a 1–0 win against Chesterfield at home and a 1–1 draw away with Chester City. Another heavy 4–0 defeat away at Burnley meant another long drive home, but at least Bobby fed us. I have always been a big believer in fate, in other words "what will be will be", and one particular incident that season made me realize how precious life is and how it can be taken away so easy.

I left my mum and dad's house in Glastonbury and headed for training in Bristol. It was a cold, icy morning and I suddenly hit a patch of black ice on Rush Hill at Farrington Gurney. The car spun around, hit a barbed wire fence and took off. It was in the days when you did not need to wear a seat belt, so I just grabbed the passenger seat and closed my eyes as the car somersaulted several times up this field, before coming to a thud, the right way up but facing up the road. As steam came out of the engine, I opened my eyes and realised that I was alive. I managed to get out and stumbled around the field. Thankfully, passing motorists stopped and called for an ambulance. It took me to Bath United Hospital, where they checked me over and dealt with my cuts and bruises. Meanwhile, the police had contacted dad to say I'd had an accident. Dad's reply was, 'are his legs okay?' which makes me laugh to this day. I was discharged, though on leaving the hospital I still felt a bit groggy, and unwittingly stumbled towards the centre of Bath. After about half an hour, I found myself sitting on a park bench feeling really unwell. I sat there and thought I'd better tell someone where I was. I continued to walk towards the centre of Bath and got to the central bus station, where I found a payphone and called dad, who then picked me up. Dad had already called Bobby Gould, who asked him to bring me to the club for the doctor to look at me. After a clean bill of health, I slept it off at home. Dad sorted out the remains of my lovely car with the local garage.

We had a game the next day, home at Exeter City, but I told Bobby I was fit to play. He partnered me up front with Archie and it paid off as we ran out 3–2 winners; Tim Parkin getting one and I got the other two. Bobby was ecstatic and told me I should crash more often. All joking aside the incident did have a real effect on me particularly in later life. Another 2–0 win followed at home to Preston, as David Williams and Archie got a goal each. Our next game away to Wimbledon turned out to be another bit of pure Bobby Gould gold. We were stuck in traffic approaching the old Plough Lane ground; it was getting closer and closer towards kick-off time and Bobby was getting more and more agitated. Suddenly, he told Kendo to stay on the coach but ordered us all off to walk the last mile of the journey. We all looked at him and he said, 'come on'. We all blindly piled off the bus and followed him. The supporters could not believe it as we got near the ground. Our party grew and grew as they joined us. By the time we got to Plough Lane, we must have had 50 fans walking with us; the Wimbledon officials thinking that we had walked from Bristol like some union demo. Bobby was in his element, even if some of us were completely bewildered by the whole thing. Kendo arrived in time to give us our kit but we lost 1–0. It certainly was a day to remember.

In the back end of the season, I only got two goals which made my tally 12 in 34 games and made me top scorer. One of those goals came in a 2–1 win away against rivals Bristol City. It was a great feeling to get one against them, particularly as they gave me such stick throughout the game. When we played them I always thought back to that time at the Hambrook hotel when they wanted to sign me. I knew I had made the right choice. City are a good club; I always loved the banter I got from their fans and I love it when I see City fans today. They give me stick but it's all done with affection on both parts. We ended the season with two wins, home to Oxford United and away at Carlisle United. We finished the season in 15th place, which was disappointing for everybody at the club. Even the relegation of neighbours City could not lift our spirits at finishing mid-table in a season where we fancied ourselves to go up after coming down the previous year. We had no luck in the cups either, losing to Fulham 2–1 at home in the FA Cup first round, and Northampton 3–1 away in the League Cup. The season ended with the high-profile transfer of my good mate, goalkeeper Martin Thomas, to Newcastle United for £50,000, which was a blow, but Phil Kite was ready to step into Tommo's shoes between the posts. The season was a bit of disappointment but if anybody could get us going next campaign, it was Bobby.

Chapter Eleven

Back on the Goal Trail

As the new season dawned, everybody at the club felt that they were going in the right direction. The 1982–83 season was to be Rovers' centenary and all of us connected with the Gas wanted to make it a special season. The directors were still pursuing their goal of getting a more secure home for us. We did not own Eastville, so they wanted to buy it from the stadium company, but in truth I don't think it was ever going to happen. The site at the M32 junction just outside the city had great links to the M4 and M5, so commercially, it was worth a fortune. The directors held talks with Bristol City and Bath City regarding ground sharing, but again it was not a popular idea amongst the fans. So their attention was turned to a greenbelt site to the north of the city at Stoke Gifford, where the directors sought planning permission for a ten million pound complex.

Bobby was wheeling and dealing. He sold Gary Mabbutt to Spurs for £105,000, which was a great move for Gary as he had bags of potential. At White Hart Lane, he won various cups and also a host of England caps, although I'm not sure whether his taste in clothes and music improved. Bobby brought in Graham Withey – a striker from Bath City – for £50,000 and another non-league signing from Bedford Town, midfielder Nicky Platnauer. Both good lads, so essentially we had kept the nucleus of the side. Our season started with an absolute disaster, losing 5–1 away to Brentford. I got on the score sheet but it still didn't stop Bobby letting us have it in the dressing room after. He certainly could dish out his own 'hairdryer' – never mind Alex Ferguson.

After the poor display at Brentford, we went on an unbeaten run of five games in which I got five goals. Things were going really well for me as Bobby was playing me up front every game, but my striking partners were changing until Bob worked out who I played better with. I had Archie and Errington Kelly, but I always played better upfront with Archie alongside me. He was a real battering ram but he could play, and with the service that Mickey Barrett was providing on the wing, everything was gelling. It was also good to see Ollie starting to get in the side. When you looked at him you knew he would give everything for the shirt. This was evident in the Gloucester Cup Final against neighbours City at the end of September. City were managed by Terry Cooper, who had gone over to the red side after his Rovers sacking, and that just added to the already fever pitch atmosphere at the game. We ran out 2–1 winners, with Ollie getting the winning goal. He was outstanding in that game. Our early form continued and we started to score for fun, dispatching the likes of Plymouth, 4–0 away, Bradford at home, 4–1, and Millwall at home, 4–1. That sort of form saw us sixth in the league midway through October.

Bobby was still wheeling and dealing; there was always a steady stream of trialists who arrived at our training ground to be given the once over by Bob. Some would play a few reserve games and some we never saw again. In October, he excelled himself with new signings. We arrived at Hambrook and Bob introduced our new forward, who was ex-England striker, Mike Channon. Mike had been a legend at Southampton, where he won the FA Cup. He had also had a big-money move to Manchester City, and was now 34 years old. He had been playing in Hong Kong before going to Newcastle United. Apparently, Bob had played with him at Southampton so he got him on a free. Talk about keeping you on your toes; Bob was a master.

Mike was a lovely bloke who is now a top racehorse trainer. You could see his love of racing even then. He was never too far away from a TV or a radio, desperate to find out how his horses were getting on. Although I was not a gambler, you couldn't help putting a few quid on one of Mike's tips. He was also really funny and I remember on one away trip, we picked him up on the way as he had been at the races, and as he sat on the coach at one of the tables, he turned to Ollie – who was only about 18 years old. He handed him a great big wedge of cash and asked Ollie to count it. I don't think Ollie had ever seen that amount. He counted it and gave it back to Mike and said; 'that's about three grand, Mike.' Mike took it back and as he put it in his pocket, Mike said; 'yeah I thought it was.' Ollie looked totally baffled and we all just fell about laughing.

Our family's favourite photo of my gorgeous sister Vinny

Always ready for a game

An early photo of the whole family

Showing promise at an early age

The mid Somerset team, thats me back row on the end, the skinny one

After signing for the Rovers with Vinny, Gail and Lorraine

A tussle with Cardiff City's Phil Dwyer on my Rovers debut at Ninian Park

Celebrating with the family after the FA Cup win against Southampton

The Randall team: Mum, Dad, Gail, Lorraine, me and Vinny
– plus dogs Lady and Tramp

Picking up the keys to my first car from the sponsor

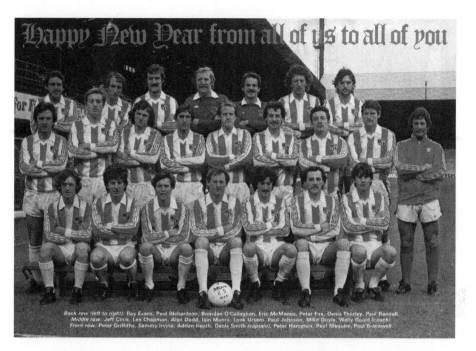

Stoke City squad photo im back row at the end on the right

After getting a last minute equaliser against Liverpool

Coming back to Rovers after signing with manager Terry Cooper and director Graham Holmes

In action for the gas

Me laughing at a photographer behind the goal. In the Bristol Rovers v Blackpool game

The remains of my lovely car after my car crash

Knocking Bristol City out of the FA Cup at Ashton Gate

Scoring for Rovers against Chelsea at Eastville

Me and Tony Pulis pre-season.
Tony is deciding how far he was going to run me

Scoring for Yeovil against Torquay

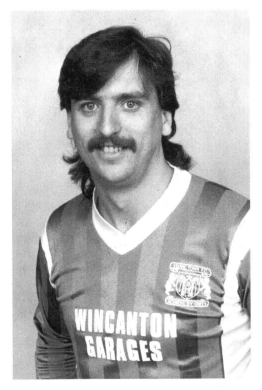

*The official photo after
signing for Yeovil Town*

At Bath City with Twerton Park behind me

Me with Mark and Kelly in Liverpool kits

Scoring a penalty for Bath City at Twerton Park

Recieving a silver salvor from Bath City Directors to mark my 100th goal for the club

Recieving the top goal scorers golden boot for Street football club from assistant manager Dad

Outside Randalls at Bath City

In the blue and white quarters of Rovers

Typical of Bob, he kept Mike on the bench as he did not want to disrupt our winning streak. We went to Leyton Orient and put on a fantastic display, winning 5–1 to send us second in the league, with goals from myself, Graham Withey who had partnered me up front, David Williams and two goals for Ollie which delighted me. Mike Channon played the next three games, replacing Ollie in Midfield as he was injured. In December, Mike left for Norwich City, where he went on to do really well, even winning the League Cup in the twilight of his career. We were still in the top half of the table but our form had become very patchy. I ended the year with 13 goals, which was still more than I had scored in the whole of last season, but I was determined to hit the 20 mark by the end of the season. With the New Year upon us, Bobby excelled himself again in the transfer market, bringing to the club one of the greatest footballers and nicest men I have ever met: Alan Ball.

Alan had just lost his job as manager of Blackpool and was looking to keep fit and get back in the game. He was a true legend and I'm not ashamed to say I was in awe of him. He had won the World Cup, had played for England 72 times and been a great player for Everton, Arsenal and Southampton. I couldn't believe he was with us. He was such a lovely man. Alan let Bobby get on with things, he did everything that Bobby asked of him and was the perfect pro. I'm sure he could have been the big I am, and to be fair we would have allowed it, considering what he achieved in the game, but no; not Bally. He was a gent.

I remember how he used to be with the apprentices; always giving them little tips to improve their game. He would muck in with all the lads. Once, we couldn't play on our so-called 'all weather' pitch at Hambrook as it was waterlogged, so we found another pitch at Eastville Park which was a couple of miles away. Bally crammed all the cones and balls into his brand new red Mercedes, and then said to the apprentices; 'right, who can drive?' As one sheepishly said he could, Bally threw him the keys and said; 'there you go, son.'

On the pitch he was a different class. I remember a game away at Wigan in the February on a terrible pitch; the rain was crashing down but Bally gave the greatest display of football that I have ever seen any player make. We won the game 5–0. His touch and passing were out of this world, and I clapped him off after the game. When I look back at that season he played with us, it was a privilege to have been on the same field as him. Now he is sadly no longer with us, I will always remember, like all those Rovers fans there that day, his display against Wigan, and the true gent he was.

Thoughts of promotion were sadly starting to fade away as we found ourselves mid-table. We had also been knocked out of the FA Cup by Plymouth Argyle, and the League Cup by Swansea City, but the Rovers fans were sticking by us and giving us great support. With this in mind, the directors decided to pay for free coaches to take the supporters to the away game at Walsall, just up the M5. It was a huge success as nearly 2,000 fans took the club up on their offer. It was a great atmosphere in the ground; trouble was, the team never read the script and we were well and truly stuffed 5–0. Bobby walked into the dressing room and ordered everybody onto the coach in 20 minutes or they would be fined a week's wages. Bobby wanted us to come out of the ground and travel down the motorway at the same time as the fans so they could give us what for. They did. Screaming and gesturing to us as we drew level with them in their coaches. It was a really difficult journey home but we deserved it. Then, as the bus stopped at Hambrook, Bobby kept us on the coach, screaming at us until we were allowed to leave at around 10pm.

The following week saw another eventful trip to my old favourite ground (I'm joking), Millwall's Den at Cold Blow Lane. Last time at the ground I got a smack from some lads who tried to nick the kit. This time, I was substitute and Bobby had a bit of a shuffle round; bringing in Tony Pulis in defence and putting Nicky Platnauer up front with Graham Withey. The game was at 1–1, with Keith Curle getting our goal. Now Keith was a great lad who went on to play at the very highest level for Manchester City and England, but back then he was still a youngster and for whatever reason, had got himself sent off. The crowd at Millwall had been giving him stick all through the game. I can only assume it was because Keith was mixed race. As the ref showed Keith the red card, the crowd went wild. In the dug out, Bobby told me to go and walk him to the dressing rooms, which were at the end of the ground. I got up and put my arm round Keith. The abuse he got was sickening; they also were throwing things at us and poor old Keith was getting more and more upset. I left him in the dressing room with Kendo, our kit man. I got back and Bobby sent me on for Graham Withey. As I had helped Keith, they all started to boo me as well. I don't know what it is with Millwall.

Our season was petering away as we finished mid-table. I had scored 20 goals, as I had hoped, but all that paled into insignificance as Bobby resigned in the May and went to manage the club he had supported as a boy, Coventry City. We were all stunned. I could understand why he wanted to take the job. Bob was torn between two clubs he loved; I know when he left the Hambrook training ground after getting his things, he was in tears. The rumours in the press were rife regarding who would be taking the job. Alan Ball was understandably top of the list, along with ex-player Larry Lloyd, who was doing a decent job at Notts County. But I'm sure none of us could foresee what the directors had in mind for the club.

Chapter Twelve

The Willo Years

With Bobby gone, there was a feeling of uncertainty at the club as to who was going to take over. Alan Ball appeared high on everyone's list, along with ex-player Larry Lloyd. But the board decided to promote from within and gave the job to midfielder David Williams, or Willo, as he was known to us. I think everybody was shocked by the appointment, I know some sections of the fans thought it was a cheap option by the board, but others – me included – thought it was a very brave decision to give him the job. He became the youngest manager in the football league at the tender age of 28. Willo had all his coaching badges and he was a very methodical type of lad. An ex-school teacher who had the respect of all the lads, he was quiet and not one of the big characters in the dressing room, which probably helped him in the transition from player to boss.

People often ask me if I can spot a future manager when I play with them. It's very difficult. For instance, Tony Pulis who is one of the country's top managers, was always going to go into management; you could see he was a good coach and really organised. Whereas, I would never have said that Ollie would also go on to have a great career in management; I just thought he was too emotionally involved to be a manager. As for Willo, yes I could see what the board saw in him – a good young prospect with ambition. He surrounded himself with good coaches too, like Pulis and Wayne Jones, another ex-player who joined as his number two. Willo's first job that summer was to give me another year on my contract, which I was only too pleased to sign. He also brought in ex-Rovers player Steve 'Chalky' White from Charlton Athletic as another option up front. I played briefly with Chalky before I went to Stoke City; he was a good lad so I was excited by the prospect. We lost Errington

Kelly, Nicky Platnauer and Graham Withey who all joined Bobby at Coventry City. I have to say, it was a surprise to most of the lads. No disrespect to those players but there were better ones Bobby could have taken – but that's Bobby to a tee, always doing the unexpected.

Willo also brought in former Bristol City 'keeper Ray Cashley, to provide experience and cover for Phil Kite. Ray was a top 'keeper and a real character; he had played in the famous City side that won promotion to the first division, but he had fallen out of favour at Ashton Gate, so it was a masterstroke by Willo to get him. Ray had no concerns about crossing from the red half to the blue half of Bristol and the supporters took to him. He was a Bristol lad who had started his career as a full-back before switching to goalkeeper. But he did have some strange ways about him, like having to make himself sick before a game due to nerves. Many a time we would go out of the tunnel, only to realise Ray was still in the toilets. He was also a nightmare if he got invited to a sponsors lounge after a game. You would go up and meet the sponsors, carrying your kit bag, but Ray's would be chinking with the sound of the bottles of wine and spirits he had somehow acquired. Many a time, as we left the room he would whisper to me; 'come on Punky, let's get going, my bag's getting heavier.'

I remember training once at Ashton Court Mansion in Bristol. We were running shuttles, which meant running slow then fast, and Cash was at the back of the group when he suddenly raced past us saying: 'I just heard something in the bushes, I think it's the gaffer'. That was Ray; always a laugh but also a bloody good 'keeper. We kicked off the season with a 2–1 defeat at Newport County. Archie got the goal after coming on as sub. My partnership with Chalky seemed like it was going to go well. I got my first goal of the season in the first home game, a 2–1 win against Southend United, and young Ollie got the other. Once we got into our rhythm, results started to happen for us, including an eight-game unbeaten run towards Christmas that saw me get three goals. But the real star was my roommate Mickey Barrett, who was flying out on the wing. Mickey had got five goals in that unbeaten run and he was starting to have probably the best season of his career. We drew Bristol City at home in the FA Cup which was fantastic. The lads were buzzing when the draw was made and the press built the game up as we were in different leagues at the time. But as we all know, the FA Cup is a great leveller. 15,000 were packed into Eastville and the atmosphere reminded me of that Southampton game all those years ago, which launched my career. City were managed by our old boss Terry Cooper and were languishing in the Fourth Division. I was paired up front with Archie while Chalky had to be content with a place on the bench. We went 1–0 up after half-time, when Archie scored a wonderful header from a Mickey Barrett cross. We were full of confidence but City replied with a goal from Tom Richie with 10 minutes to go. Then, with literally the last kick of the match, Martyn Hirst scored to make it 2–1 to City. It was a real blow and one that still hurts to this day. As we ended the year we were eighth in the league. Willo liked to keep a settled side, which I have to admit we were not used to at Eastville. He rotated the striking partners with myself, Archie, Chalky and a new signing called Paul Bannon from Carlisle United. Willo's activity in the transfer market did not end there as he sold our keeper Phil Kite to Southampton for £50,000, which was good business for all concerned – especially as we had Cash waiting in the wings. It was a great opportunity for Kitey to play at a higher level.

As we entered the New Year, I was still finding goals hard to come by but Pulis and Jono were excellent coaches. They encouraged me and told me that I was working hard for the team. Call me old fashioned, but I wanted goals, as that was my game. The season petered out for us even though we finished fifth, which, nowadays would put you in the play-offs. The one memorable moment for me at the end of that season was the last game away at Hull City. We were booked into the Swallow Hotel for a pre-match meal in South Normanton, which was about 80 miles from Hull's Boothferry Park. When we got there, Liverpool FC were also booked in and tucking into their pre-match meal before their game at Nottingham Forest. All their great players were there: Rush, Dalgliesh, Hansen – I was like a kid on seeing them, as we all knew Liverpool was my club.

We had our meal then boarded the bus, only to find that it wouldn't start. The battery was as flat as a pancake. Willo told us to stay on the bus and change into our kits, and as we did, the Liverpool lads came out and boarded their bus, which was next to ours. God knows what they must have thought of this ramshackle bunch changing on the coach, I don't think I have ever been so embarrassed. Picture the scene: there I was with Kenny Dalgliesh and co staring at me and the lads in our underpants. Willo decide that we would order a fleet of taxis to the game so we paired up and I got Cashley with me in my taxi. Just outside Hull we got a blowout. The driver pulled over to the side so Cash and I helped him change the wheel.

Can you imagine the sight, two Bristol Rovers players in full kit at the side of the road changing a wheel, as all the Rovers supporters' coaches went past, beeping their horns and waving? The game kicked off 15 minutes late but the fact that we drew 0–0 after all that still amazes me to this day.

My tally for the season was only six goals and that meant I was not the leading scorer at the club. To be leading scorer meant everything to me but I was pleased for Archie, who topped it with 13 goals, closely followed by Mickey Barrett, Chalky, and Brian Williams who all had nine goals to their name. I was determined to put it right the following season. Willo did not do much in the transfer market the following season as he appeared happy with us lads, after a top five finish. His style was so different to Bobby's, who seemed to have trialists arriving all the time. The only business he did do was selling Tony Pulis to Newport County for £8,000. I loved Tony to bits but I wouldn't miss those long runs and him telling me about my weight every summer.

The coaching staff still worked us hard over the summer with runs and it was a real shock that Mickey Barrett was struggling. Now Mickey was one of the fittest lads at the club and had just come off the back of one of his best seasons in the league, but he was lagging behind everyone in the runs and that was certainly not Mickey. I said to him, 'are you okay mate?' and he just said he felt a bit rough. He went to see the club doctor, who sent him to a specialist at the Bristol Royal Infirmary. The specialist diagnosed Mickey with cancer and he was dead within two weeks. Apparently the cancer had spread through his whole body and there was nothing that could be done. We could not believe it; he was 24 years old and married with a baby on the way. The whole club was in shock. It is times like that when you are proud of your own football club. Everybody rallied round and helped each other, from tea lady to directors. We had already had one tragedy when defender Tim Parkin had lost a son and now we had lost one of our brightest stars. I carried Mickey's coffin along with Ollie, Archie, Aidan McCaffrey, Brian Williams and Willo. It was a terrible day that I will never forget. The club arranged a benefit game for his family, against

Aston Villa, and the fans responded as the Gas Heads always do, by coming to the match in their thousands. Mickey's dad still came and watched the Rovers and to this day, I don't know how he found the strength to do that. It was a privilege to have him there.

When I look back, I think about what a terrible loss it was. Mickey was destined for great things in football and I think he would have played for England. He was a wonderful lad; God bless you, mate! We did not have the best preparation for the season but we did feel we owed it to Mickey to have a good season. Willo did some more wheeling and dealing in the transfer market, bringing forward Mark O'Connor to the club from QPR for a cut price of £20,000. We also had a young lad called Gary Penrice from the youth team. He never stopped moaning and some training sessions I did my best to kick the fuck out of him. Pen was a very gifted footballer who went on to be a great player for Rovers, Watford and QPR. He had no respect for the older pros and would try and put the ball between their legs in training, and believe me, you only did that once against the likes of Aidan McCaffery, but that was also part of Pen's charm.

We hit the ground running, going unbeaten in our first seven games. I was on fire with four goals to my name. As we got into November, we hit a bit of a blip, going down 3–2 at Plymouth Argyle and losing 3–0 against newly promoted neighbours Bristol City at Ashton Gate. We were also going great guns in the League Cup, beating Swindon Town 5–1 at the County Ground. I got two that night, it was one of my best ever performances in the blue and white quarters. Our reward was to be drawn against Arsenal in a two-legged affair, the first leg being at Highbury. It was a tremendous experience for all of us to walk into the marbled halls of Highbury with the underfloor heating in the changing room. Maybe some of the lad's minds remained in the changing rooms, as we lost 4–0. Yet we redeemed ourselves in the second leg, holding a strong Arsenal side 1–1 at Eastville, with Chalky getting our goal. In the FA Cup, we drew part-timers King's Lynn, which was always going to be a banana skin if we let it. After going a goal down, we got ourselves together and scraped through 2–1. Our prize this time was an away draw at Bristol City, who had demolished us in the league 3–0 a week earlier, so there were massive groans at the training ground when we heard the draw.

Ashton Gate was packed for this Bristol derby. City were well up for it, especially as they went ahead after only four minutes. We just looked at each other, thinking, 'oh no, not again', but Mark O'Connor got one back, then on 18 minutes I was put through with the 'keeper to beat, and I stuck it home to put us 2–1 up. Then, just before half-time I was put through again. I outpaced my old mate Keith Curle who had joined City via Torquay United a year earlier, and I rounded the keeper and put us 3–1 up to knock City out of the cup. The scenes afterwards were fantastic; all my mates joined me and dad in the players' bar at City and after various renditions of '*Goodnight, Irene*' and '*One Nil Down, Three One Up, We Knocked City Out The Cup*', we made our way home to Glastonbury to sleep off a tremendous night for the club. When I got home to my mum and dad's, my sister Gail was out on a date with a lad who supported City. He refused to come into the house knowing I was there, as he couldn't face me following my two goals.

We eventually got knocked out in the following round by Ipswich Town, who beat us 2–1 at Portman Road, with Ollie getting our goal. It wasn't a great cup run but that win at City will stay with me forever. It was like the Southampton win all over again. We had a shock at Christmas, as Archie was sold to Middlesbrough for a bargain £20,000. Also, midfielder Geraint Williams found himself moving to Derby County for £40,000 as Willo balanced the books. I missed Archie – he was a good partner for me and we were very much alike, coming through non-league football, but the move to Middlesbrough was a dream for him so I wished him all the best.

I was still on fire and ended the year with 15 goals. Willo had decided to keep me up front and my partners were mainly Paul Bannon and Chalky. I enjoyed playing with either of them as we all gave everything for the cause. Although, in an away game at Doncaster I almost gave a little bit too much. The game was on a Friday night, which worked out perfect for me as my sister Lorraine was getting married on the Saturday, so there was no awkward decision for me to make. Though I have to be honest and say that I would have risked a club fine if it was the Saturday; I would not have missed that wedding for the world. We were drawing 2–2, with our goals coming from Parkin and O'Connor. I was put through to chase a ball, with their keeper coming out as well. As we reached each other, he caught me with his studs in what can only be described as my meat and two veg. Now any bloke reading this will know how that pain feels. Never mind childbirth (that's a joke). Well, I was on the floor with the physio, Roy Dolling, stood over me. Blood started to spread across my white shorts and you did not need to be a physio to work out what was bleeding. They put me on a stretcher and carried me off the pitch. I passed the Rovers fans who were all waving, but their faces changed as I got nearer to them and they could see what I had injured. I think every bloke I went past pulled a face.

I bandaged myself up and got on the coach home. The next day at the wedding I was walking around like John Wayne; relatives even asked me if I had been horse riding the day before. But the meat and two veg healed and my kids, Mark and Kelly, are testimony to the fact that everything works down below. Our season continued, with us not really being able to get a run together and, typical of Rovers at that time, we faded away yet again and finished sixth in the league. My own tally was 18 goals in 43 matches, which meant I reclaimed the leading scorer title at the club. As I said, it was a title that was very dear to my heart. That was my job at Rovers, to score goals, and that's what a striker is judged by. Before the season ended, full-back Neil Slater was sold to Oxford United for £80,000, and Ollie decided a move would be better for his career so he went to Wimbledon for £40,000 – both moves resulting in a healthy profit for the directors. I could understand Ollie moving; he had a great season at the club and as we all know, he went on to bigger and better things. But we all know he is a Gas Head at heart. The most incredible transfer of the season was that Willo sold himself to Norwich City for £40,000, leaving us without a great midfielder and, more importantly, a manager. It was a great move for him because he went on to have success at Carrow Road as a player. He also went on to establish himself as a coach with Leeds United and Manchester United. I wonder what we might have achieved with Willo if he had stayed. After all, in his two seasons in charge, we had been top six in both. In the meantime, the Rovers board would spend the summer looking for yet another manager.

Chapter Thirteen

Falling Out of Love

The board at Bristol Rovers certainly had their work cut out in the summer of 1985. Not only did the plans to build a new stadium at Stoke Gifford fall through, but they also had to find a new manager. In the end, the appointment of a new manager did not seem that difficult. A certain boss was free due to his Coventry City side sacking him after a disappointing 5–1 defeat to local rivals Leicester City. So Rovers' new manager was Bobby Gould.

The appointment of Bobby would turn out to be directors Barry Bradshaw and Martin Flook's last act in charge, as they resigned due to the lack of progress in finding a new ground. They sold their shares to Geoff Dunford and Roy Redman, both local businessmen and more importantly, Rovers fans. The lads were quite happy that Bobby was coming back; we knew him and he knew the majority of us so we never really saw any massive changes at the club. We were all quite excited to see if Bobby could build on the good work done by Willo and maybe get us out of this division. Bobby arrived and decided that due to Rovers' ever-increasing money woes, he was going to go with youth this season, a move that saw highly paid Ray Cashley, Aidan McCaffery and Brian Williams – amongst others – leave the club.

I was sad to see the lads go. Ray, in particular, was a real character in the dressing room. I did think it was probably for the best, as it would only have been a matter of time before he and Bobby had clashed. Bobby brought in a load of new players. In our first league game of the season, away at Darlington, we fielded no fewer than five debutants. I played up front with Gary Penrice who was still the same annoying youngster, but he was a real talent. We played well in a thrilling 3–3 draw, but myself and Pen couldn't find the net. A lad called Steve Baddock did score on his debut for us. Steve was on a part-time contract as he worked for British Rail. That was typical of Bobby; he kept finding players for the club. He was the type of boss that as quick as he found them, if it didn't work out he would let them go, and that's what happened to Steve. He played a few games for us but Bobby got rid of him later in the season to Gloucester City.

Bobby kept faith with the same side for our first home game against Brentford, but a poor performance saw us lose 1–0. I lost my place up front to Chalky for the next three games. I was angry but that was football, and I was sure I would get my chance. In that spell I played for the reserves, run by Harold Jarman, a real Rovers legend. H, as he was known, was a brilliant winger for Rovers in their golden period of the 1950s and 60s, and I loved him to bits. I got the goal-scoring boots on, scoring four in three reserve games, and H would pat me on the back and say, with fag hanging out of his mouth, 'well done, Punky'. In September, Bobby brought Gerry Francis to the club as player-coach. Gerry, as we all know, was a great player for QPR and England. He had been playing around the lower leagues and had come to us from Exeter City. Bobby wanted Gerry to do some of the coaching, and I have to say he was a revelation. His coaching methods were brilliant; the players really took to the sessions. He was a real help to the new nucleus of youngsters we had at the club at that time.

We also suffered a goalkeeping crisis at the club as we had no cover for keeper Ron Green. Typical of Bobby, he got his mate, ex-Arsenal keeper Bob Wilson, to come out of retirement and train with us. He also made sure Bob brought a camera crew with him as Wilson was hosting the BBC show *Football Focus* at the time. They filmed us taking shots at Wilson but in the end nothing came of Wilson joining. That was typical of Gouldy, he loved to get Rovers publicity and to his credit, it worked as the footage was shown the following week on *Football Focus*.

I forced my way back into the side for the away game at Swansea City; this time partnering another new signing, Trevor Morgan. He was a £15,000 signing from Exeter City. We seemed to work well together and Trevor scored in a 1–0 win for us. Our partnership continued through to October where we were beaten away, 6–1 at Bournemouth, with me getting our consolation goal. Bobby was furious; we knew we had let ourselves down. Bobby decided to keep us on the coach again while he let us have it at the training ground until late into the night. We were struggling as a side, winning only three games out of 15. But whereas Willo had kept a settled team, Bobby was changing things round and bringing in trialists all the time as well as relying heavily on the youngsters at the club. I knew I wasn't in great form but I did not think getting two in 12 league games and five in five cup games was that bad. Bobby obviously did, dropping me to the bench for the next game and replacing me with Pen. I then found myself in the reserves with H, who was really supportive and told me all I had to do was get Bobby to notice me again. It was clear now that I had moved down the pecking order behind Trevor Morgan, Chalky and Pen, and it was a bit reminiscent of my time at Stoke City. So I did what I did there and got my head down. I was not the type to go banging on Bobby's door, as I would rather show him in training and in the reserves that I was still a good player.

I played six reserve games up to the end of the year and scored ten goals but still there was no chance in the first team for me. The first team were still indifferent and we were still sat in the bottom half of the table come January.

Suddenly I got a call to Bobby's office. He told me that there had been an enquiry from a Dutch first division club called NAC Breda. Their manager Bob Maaskant wanted to speak to me with a view to going for a trial and a possible contract. I asked Bobby what he thought and he said it would be good for me. From that moment I knew that maybe my time at Rovers was coming to an end. I spoke to Bob Maaskant and he told me that I had been recommended to him by Paul Bannon, who had left us to join NAC Breda. The club was based just outside of Rotterdam in the north of Holland. I agreed to go and he said he would sort out the tickets and accommodation. My family was really supportive about me going. It meant a lot to me knowing I had their support. Dad drove me to Bristol Airport on the Monday morning, for my week's trial in Holland. When I got to the airport, every flight was fog bound and the airline was making arrangements to take the passengers to Gatwick. I sat there and thought long and hard about my Dutch adventure. Was I running away? I also believed that I was good enough to force my way back in the side, as I had not become a bad player overnight. All these thoughts were spinning around in my head. As the time grew nearer and nearer for me to board the coach for Gatwick, I made the decision to get in a taxi and come back home.

I arrived back in my mum and dad's house and when my dad got home from work, to say he looked surprised to see me was an understatement. We talked about my future; dad could see I was unhappy at being left out but he said he would support me whatever I did. I called Bobby and told him about the fog and how I had decided to stay and fight for my place. He just said okay, so I called Bob Maaskant and apologised for my absence but he understood. I returned to more reserve football at Rovers. I was so used to it now that me and H would pick the team, him with fag in mouth, saying 'what about him at right-back, Punky?' Although I enjoyed training with the first team and H, I was desperate to get in the first team. I played for Rovers reserves right up to March. I had scored 18 goals for them in 20 games, which was phenomenal in anybody's book. Although it can be soul destroying playing for the reserves, I never complained, I just got on with it. I remember a game against Plymouth Argyle when I had put us 1–0 up after the interval. Then our young 'keeper Tim Carter got injured. H put me in goal. I was diving about shot stopping. One shot I caught in the midriff. It winded me so I just walked round the six-yard box bouncing the ball until I got my breath back. Everyone was shouting 'get on with it'. But we got a win in the end. After my exploits at Plymouth, I found myself in the team against Swansea City at home. Trevor Morgan was injured, and I was delighted. Bobby just said, 'you're in against Swansea'. I must admit, it was like playing my debut all over again. The fans were fantastic. They were singing my name, and it was really touching to know they had not forgotten me. I played up front with Chalky, and although we had a few chances, the game ended 0–0.

Trevor was still injured for the following game away at Notts County so I kept my place. We again drew 0–0. Trevor returned and I never even made the bench for the next game, forcing me back to the reserves. Rovers were still struggling at the wrong end of the table. Bobby brought in another pair of recruits from Leeds United; a defender, John Scales, and striker David Mehew. Both would go on to have glittering careers at Rovers but I knew it was the beginning of the end for me. I had been left out before at Stoke but there was always that thought that you might get back in with Rovers. It was plain that no matter what I did – or my 18 goals in the reserves – Bobby just did not fancy me in the side. I had never felt like this before. Even when I was a kid getting rejections from different clubs, one thing was always there; I loved football. But now I was starting to fall out of love with the one thing that had been my life. I thought long and hard, and I decided to draft up a transfer request, something that I thought I would never do. But I felt I needed a change, and maybe a new challenge. It was so difficult because this was Bristol Rovers. I did not care about leaving Bobby, I cared about asking to leave the club – my club, the club that had looked after me and given me a chance in the game, the club where the fans sang my name on my debut at Cardiff City and where teammates gave me a nickname that lasted my whole life. The club where I had made the national papers as the supermarket kid in the FA Cup. The club where I had carried the coffin of one of my teammates. The club I loved.

I handed the transfer request to Bobby and he just took it and I left his office. There were all sorts of rumours regarding clubs coming in for me, notably Bristol City, but nothing happened. Then, out of the blue, Bobby told me non-league Yeovil Town were interested in signing me. Their manager, ex-Bristol City midfielder Gerry Gow, and chairman Gerry Locke were keen to come down and talk to me. I was a bit surprised that no league club had come in for me; after all I was 28 years old and I had scored regularly for Rovers and Stoke. Maybe my details had not been circulated enough to other clubs? But I will never know.

To go and play non-league would be a massive decision. It would mean I would have to find a job and my only qualifications were scoring goals. After talking it through with my dad, I thought; 'sod it, I will give it a go'. I met Gerry Gow and Yeovil chairman Gerry Locke at the Rovers training ground. Both clubs agreed a £5,000 fee for a two-year deal, which would be worth £120 a week to me plus £20 win and £10 draw bonuses. They also said they could find me a job at the club which would make up my money. I signed and at that moment, Gerry Gow picked up the phone and told the local press: 'you won't believe this but we have signed Paul Randall!'

I said my goodbyes to all the staff, and to his credit, Bobby wished me well. Thinking back, it's funny remembering that conversation we both had under a tree at the Hambrook training ground all those years ago, when he joined as a player. He asked me what I was going to do when I finished playing. Little did I know, he would have a big part in ending my league career. I have no real bitterness towards Bobby. Mainly due to the fact that I am not that sort of bloke. I respected him as my manager; I know it was a difficult time for the club and he relied heavily on the youngsters who came good for him in the end. So off I went into the non-league and a new challenge at Hewish Park.

Chapter Fourteen

Do You Know Who I Am?

Throughout my life family has been the most important thing to me, even more than football. I don't think I have ever made a footballing decision without thinking of the impact on those around me. Football being the game it is, you don't always have a say in what will happen to you. But when I did, family came first. I will always remember being asked by an employer a couple of years ago, 'what's your five-year plan, Paul? What's your ambition?' I had no hesitation in saying; 'I played football for a living at a high level; I have a beautiful wife and two lovely kids. To be honest I have achieved every ambition I ever had. Work will always just be work.'

My wife Filomena, or Fil as she is always known, has been the love of my life for over 25 years. We first met in 1983 when I was playing for Rovers. I went into a pub in Glastonbury called The Market House, for a few drinks with my mates. I stood at the bar and noticed a group of friends I knew over the other side of the room. In amongst them was Fil. I turned to my mates and said; 'cor she's alright. Who is she?' They told me that her name was Filomena Esposito; she was a friend of one of the group. Apparently Fil also asked the group she was with; 'who's he?' and they replied, 'you don't want to know him'. Obviously my reputation for the ladies had followed me from Stoke. Both groups met up later that evening at the local nightclub in Glastonbury called Brewster's. And it was there that the title of this chapter was born.

Fil always says that I approached her that night and said those cringewor-thy words; 'Do you know who I am?' I vehemently deny this as I have never said that, ever, mainly due to the fact that I would never use a corny line like that. We got chatting and arranged to meet up the next day. Unbeknown to me, Fil invited her mates just in case I didn't show up. I did show up and so her mates left us alone together. She really was beautiful, with dark hair and a fabulous figure. Her mum and dad had moved from Naples in the 1960s to find a better life for her and her brother and sister. There was even a football connection, as her dad Antonio had once had a trial for Juventus back in the 1950s as a goalie. I really did think I had hit the jackpot. Fil worked in Wells at Claire's as a machinist. Claire's was a factory making sheepskin clothes and a big employer at the time.

We got on really well; she had no interest in sport of any kind, which I quite liked as we could talk about all sorts of things and not about the sitter I may have missed on Saturday. I don't know if it was my immaturity or just that I wasn't ready to have a girlfriend at that time but I was a dreadful boyfriend. I wouldn't turn up to dates and I just loved being with my mates so we just drifted apart and went our separate ways. I just carried on with my life, while Fil, after a time, got engaged and was ready to buy a house with her fiancée. We met again in the summer of 1985 at a wedding do for mutual friends at Glastonbury town hall. She had broken off her engagement and I think I just cheered her up that night. We talked and talked and that was when I thought she might be the one. I realised that I had let her go once before and I wasn't going to let it happen again. We started to see each other regularly; she would stay over at my house now and again but when I dropped her off at her house her dad would always be at the curtain looking to see who this lad was who had started to go out with his daughter. I remember I usually parked around the corner to pick Fil up so she wouldn't get interrogated by her protective father. But this night I parked outside. As Fil was upstairs getting ready, her mum and dad invited me in for coffee, to give me the once over as a prospective son-in-law. Fil's face was a picture when she came down the stairs and saw me sat between her mum and dad on the settee. I could understand her dad being the way he was; he was just looking out for her. I obviously passed the test, as I never sat outside in the car again.

About three months into the relationship, we sat outside her house and I said to her; 'Don't you get fed up with me dropping you off like this?' and she yes.

'Well let's do something about it then and get married,' I said.

She said yes and we were married 14 June 14 1986 on a hot sunny day at Wells. It was a fantastic day, Fil looked gorgeous and both families came together – Scousers and Italians. Both sets of cultures are family oriented so that has stayed with us to this day. My best man was my sister Vinny's husband, Dave, who himself is Italian. We had a reception at the Swan Hotel in Wells. It must have been quite daunting for Fil, entering the family, but she got on great. She was also fantastic with my mum and dad and I think they were pleased to see me settle down at last. After the wedding, we didn't have a honeymoon, we just all went down the pub on the Sunday.

Fil and I moved into a lovely three-bedroom house at Paradise Road in Glastonbury. My bachelor lifestyle had officially come to an end, not before time some might say. Fil became pregnant in the September. We were both overjoyed. I had joined Yeovil Town and was playing part-time. Although we did not know how things would work out in terms of my career, at least we were local and near friends and family. I was part-time for Yeovil and I worked as a labourer with my brother-in-law Norm, who had started up his own building business. It was on one of his sites that I got the call to say Fil had gone into labour. I raced home and bundled her into the car to take her to the maternity suite at Taunton Hospital. She was in a great deal of pain and I was no help. I was so excited to be a dad, that as I drove along Glastonbury High Street and saw an old mate called Dave McCartney, I wound down the window and shouted; 'Here we go, here we go, here we go', much to Fil's annoyance. She told me to shut up and get her to hospital. Dave later told me he thought I was off to a football match.

Mark was born May 1987; after a few scares at the birth when the umbilical cord got stuck around his neck, he was fit and healthy. I cannot describe the feeling of being a dad; it was like no other I had ever had. I was so proud. Fil and I decided on the name Mark as we both liked it, so off I went to make the phone calls to tell our mums and dads that they were now grandparents. Our daughter Kelly was born in the November the following year; it seemed that if I only looked at Fil she would get pregnant. Our Randall family was now complete. To get a daughter was wonderful; we couldn't have been happier and considered ourselves very lucky indeed.

Even though I was relatively well known through the football, I wasn't rolling in money and at times things were hard, especially with two young kids, but I always did what my mum and dad had done, to try and give them the best childhood I could. Having a son was always going to bring outside pressure onto mine and Mark's relationship. I wish I had a pound for the number of people who said, 'I bet he will be a footballer like his dad'. I knew he loved football from an early age; after all, it was all around him. I remember one Christmas when he and two of his cousins had a remote control car each. Mark kicked a balloon up and down the house all Christmas Day, and no matter how many times we said; 'play with your car, Mark', he just wanted the balloon.

Again, when he was around 10 years old, I took him and some of his friends to King Alfred School at Burnham-on-Sea, to a football training night that Bristol City were holding, so they could look at youngsters. After three weeks, the City coaches would read out names of the lads that they wanted to see the following weeks. Mark was on the list but some of his mates were not. I will never forget the look on the faces of those young lads on the way home; some of them were crying in the car they were so disappointed. I remember thinking it wasn't the right way to do things. Fortunately for me, Mark looked up at me and said, 'dad, I don't want to go anymore'. I could have kissed him. I never wanted to see him disappointed like that, especially at 10 years old. I am glad he felt he could tell me how he felt, even at that early age, and not feel he was letting me down. It seems a Randall was never destined to play for the red half of Bristol after all.

Today, Mark plays left-back for Wells City. He has played at county level and has a wonderful left foot; something that people often tell me I never had. Mark loves his football and I always encourage him but never push him. As long as he's happy, that's all that matters. He is learning to be a butcher and I am so proud of him, as he is making his own way in life and I get such a kick out of me and my dad watching him play on a Saturday. Especially when I hear dad shout out the same things to him that he used to shout at me.

I am also incredibly proud of Kelly. She, like Mark, is sport-mad and plays netball and rounders. She has represented her county at netball and I couldn't be more proud of her. I used to see a lot of Lorraine and me in the way that Mark and Kelly would play and fight. They always looked out for each other in much the same way Lorraine and I did. Kelly is also a lot like my mum in respect of: leave a job Friday and start a new one Monday. I just don't know how she does it, but she is great with people and they take to her. I have no idea what she will end up doing – I don't think she does – but as long as she's happy.

As you can tell, sport has always played a massive part in our lives. I remember when the kids were younger, and me and Fil would take them to Cornwall on holiday and there would be me, Mark and Kelly playing some kind of game while Fil sat on the sun-lounger reading a book. She was the same when I met her and she hasn't changed; she just hates it. As the kids are growing up now, we have a real sense of family about us. That was severely put to the test when my wonderful sister Vinny was killed. We were all there for each other. I know that Fil, Mark and Kelly helped me through some very difficult times in that period. They knew when to leave me alone and let me have my space and when I needed to talk about things. I knew it was difficult for them, as they had lost a sister-in-law and an auntie so they also were grieving. Fil was fantastic with my mum and dad, giving them love and support.

I know the chapter started on a light note with the famous quote; 'Do you know who I am?' Well I will answer the question. I am Paul Randall and I am incredibly lucky to have two fantastic kids and an amazing wife who I love with all my heart.

Chapter Fifteen

A New Challenge

Yeovil Town was a massive club in non-league terms, when I signed for them midway through the 1985–86 season. The club is steeped in history, mainly for their FA Cup exploits, particularly when they knocked the mighty Sunderland out of the tournament in the 1940s on the famous sloping Huish Park pitch.

I had played on the pitch in a couple of county games when I was younger and yes, it did slope – 17 feet apparently, from one end to the other. It had become part of the folklore at the club. The club are called The Glovers, due to the glove-making industry in the town. They were in the Vauxhall Opel Premier Division after being relegated from the conference the previous season. Straight away, I got the feeling that from fan to director, the club was desperate to get into the football league. The crowds the clubs were getting were unbelievable for that division – averaging around the 2,000 to 3,000 mark. Everything about them was geared for success. The set up was, in parts, better than I had experienced at Bristol Rovers. We travelled by coach to games and stayed overnight in hotels that most league clubs would have been happy to stay in. The dressing room also was full of ex-pros and promising youngsters.

Off the field, the board was in the process of negotiating the sale of the old Huish Park and relocating to a new ground. I had heard all this stuff before at my time at Rovers, but this really did seem like it was going to happen. Chairman Gerry Locke, who was a local businessman, had installed manager Gerry Gow towards the end of the previous season when relegation was a foregone conclusion. This was Gerry's first full season to show what he could do. Gerry Gow was a tough, no-nonsense midfielder who was a legend with the Bristol City fans. He played in the promotion side of 1976 and led City's midfield in the top flight before being transferred to Manchester City, where he played in the FA Cup Final for them against Spurs. I think anybody who remembers that match will also remember Gerry's tackle in the first minute on Argentinean star Osvaldo Ardiles, which left the Spurs midfielder on the ground in agony. Gerry had let him know that he was in for a long afternoon. Gerry then moved to Burnley and then on to Yeovil where he was player manager; it looked like exciting times ahead.

When I arrived, the club was near the top of the league and fighting it out with leaders Sutton United. We had some good lads in the dressing room, many with league experience, like Tom Richie who had played for Bristol City and at one point was rumoured to have been swapped with me when I was at Stoke City. Dave Linney was there, who I had been at Rovers with in my first spell at Eastville, and Jon Economou was another ex-Bristol City lad. Plus there were some new lads like Alan Pardew who had come from Dulwich Hamlet for £5,000 and Tony Ricketts, a £10,000 buy from rivals Bath City. Added to this, my new strike partner; a lad called John McGinley.

John had been picked up from Scotland, and although not very big at around five foot nine, his timing in the air was perfection, and we developed a real partnership on and off the field. The club was as good as their word and sorted me out a job in the commercial department under the guidance of the commercial manager, ex-Bristol City and Arsenal player Alan Skirton, along with Dave Linney and Secretary Betty Hall. It really did show how forward thinking they were at Yeovil at the time. They were exploring different ways to bring cash into the club and it's something that today's clubs do all the time, but back then not many professional clubs did it, let alone part-time clubs.

Our jobs would be to go around and canvass local residents and business-es, getting them to buy scratch and lottery cards with a percentage going to the club. Or with the local companies; getting them to sponsor games or put money into the club. This, Dave and I would do, while fitting in training twice a week. I did find it hard to adjust to normal life but that was what part-time football was all about. On the pitch, I made my debut the day after signing for the club, away at leaders Sutton United. We lost 3–1, with Jon McGinley get-ting our goal. I was disappointed to lose the game and not score but I knew I wasn't really match fit, and the signs were that we had a really good side. I was also impressed with the standard of the football in the division.

Gerry let off a bit of steam in the dressing room after, saying we had not done ourselves justice and we had let them get further away from us in the league. It also ended our 20-match undefeated run. I did think, 'Oh Christ, I join and the club gets beat', but we could put it right on Tuesday with another away game against bottom of the league, Hendon. I got my first goal in the green and white of Yeovil in that away game at Hendon. It came after 15 minutes. Alan Pardew crossed and I just turned the ball into the net. It is always great to score and I did not want people thinking I had lost my touch. That's why that night at Hendon, in front of around 150 people, that goal meant as much to me as any of the ones I scored in the top flight. It might as well have been Anfield in my mind; it still felt the same. We won the game 2–1 with Alan Pardew getting the winner. From a personal point of view, my play up front with Jon McGinley made me feel like we were going to do well together.

I got another two goals the following Saturday at Huish Park as we beat Epsom and Ewell 3–0. The supporters gave me a great ovation after the game, which meant a lot to me. Following the win, we had to play Bristol City at Huish Park on the Wednesday night in the Somerset Premier Cup semi-final. I couldn't wait to come up against the old enemy as it were, and I was sure the City fans would be up for giving me a bit of stick. Huish had around 1,500 inside it to see if we could beat them. Admittedly, City would field a combination of youth and reserve players but also a few first teamers, but it never made any difference to us as it was still Bristol City and we would give our all to beat them and get to a Cup Final. I got the usual stick from the City fans in the warm up but it was all banter. And I'm sure they were not happy come the end, as we beat them 4–2, with yours truly getting another two goals to send us to a two-legged final with bitter rivals Bath City later in the season.

Unfortunately for us, we lost the first leg of the Final 1–0 at Twerton Park, and then went down 2–0 at home in the second leg, losing 3–0 on aggregate – so it was a loser's medal for me. What struck me about the games against Bath City was the intense bitter rivalry both clubs had for each other. Now I had played in the Bristol derby, which could be a bit tasty at times, but this was mental. Both sets of supporters really did dislike each other. It was as fierce as any rivalry between league clubs.

In the league we were chasing Sutton, and towards the end of the season we played them at Huish, beating them 2–0 with goals from John McGinley and Dave Spencer, in front of an amazing 5,500 supporters. The attendance really showed what this club could do if we ever got in the conference, let alone the football league. Unfortunately we just couldn't catch Sutton as they won the league with 95 points and we finished second with 91 points. I had played 14 games and netted seven goals, which I thought was not bad. Gerry had done a good job at the club; he had used his skill on and off the field to get people talking about the club again and that would mean that next season we could really push on.

The summer was much the same for me; keeping fit with the lads at Glastonbury and doing my own running work when I could. Off the pitch, there was big upheaval for me as I was getting married in the June. I was also working through the summer with the commercial department, trying to get the public and businesses signed up to support the club. This meant that I was going all over the area, knocking on doors and cold-calling clients to get them interested. When the new season arrived, Gerry had been given a bit of cash to spend and he brought in forward Carl Zachhau from Walthamstow for £3,000, as well as full-back Phil Fearns from Aldershot, without showing too many players the door. Carl hit the ground running, getting a hat-trick in the season showpiece; the charity shield game which was traditionally between the team that won the cup and the team that had won the league. As Sutton had won both, they played us who had finished second. We won the game 5–1 on a hot August afternoon, and won Yeovil's first trophy for ten years.

In September, I got my first goal of the new season in a 1–1 draw away at Workington Town. The club went undefeated that month, sending us to the top of the table and earning the Manager of the Month award for Gerry. I found goals hard to get by my standards. I had hit only four goals in the first few months of the season, a run which prompted Gerry to drop me to the reserves. That did not bother me to be honest, as I was just happy to play. I felt that with me being dropped, some of the pressure had been lifted off me that I had experienced in league football. I had no problems turning out for the reserves, especially if we struggled to get a side. Reserve team football did me the world of good. I found my scoring boots again, getting goals in every game I played. Gerry responded in typical style by saying; 'wish you could fucking do that in the league'. The club was busy in the transfer market towards the end of October, bringing in ex-Bristol City youngster Ricky Chandler and also City youngster Mickey Tanner on loan, and we went on a bit of a run, beating non-league rivals Wycombe Wanderers 4–1 in the AC Delco Cup. But a spell of 12 wins in 13 matches came to a halt as we lost 1–0 at home to Croydon. That defeat, along with three successive 1–1 draws, made the success-hungry supporters vent their anger towards Gerry. Citing personal problems, he resigned – at which we were all shocked. The supporters demanded league football and at that time, I think they felt that he could not deliver it.

Footballers are all the same, whether they are pros or part-timers; rumours do the rounds when a manager is sacked, but really, they are not bothered and just get on with it. And it was no different at Huish Park. There were the usual applicants, one of whom was my old horseracing tipster from Bristol Rovers, ex-England player Mike Channon – and who could blame him? Yeovil was one of the top jobs in non-league football. Surprisingly, the board went with Brian Hall, a 47-year-old police trainer from London. Hall had played at Southern League level and was a fully qualified coach who had worked with various clubs in the non-league scene, mainly in and around the London area. I remember the first time I set eyes on him. He marched on to the training ground with a clipboard and I remember thinking; 'what the fuck have we got here'. But to give him his due, Brian was meticulous in his preparation and homework and he certainly got us organized, although he did clash at times with John McGinley, as no matter what he wanted us to do, John would always do his own thing. He also brought a lot of lads in from London clubs that he knew; lads like Steve Rutter, Paul Millar and Gary Donnellan, who all did well for the Glovers. Hall generated a bit of cash as well by selling Alan Pardew to Crystal Palace for £7,000; a move that set Alan on the road to the great career he has had in the game. I changed career also, leaving the commercial department and joining my brother-in-law Norm in his building business as a labourer. The commercial job was good but it just was not me; I was never really comfortable with the cold calling and the knocking on doors the job required. I also knew the building work would keep me fit.

Brian would not find his first league victory until February, with a 2–1 win at home, with me and Paul Millar getting our goals. That result certainly calmed the supporters down, who were starting to get restless with our recent results. We were still chasing Wycombe Wanderers in the league and it looked like it was going to be a frustrating second place for us again. In the non-league cups, we were beaten 4–0 on aggregate by Hendon in the Delco Cup semi-final, which was a real blow for us. We had also got to the semi-final of the Somerset Premier Cup again, and were drawn with rivals Bath City. We drew 1–1 at home in the first leg, then drew 1–1 again after extra time at Twerton Park, sending the tie to another game at Twerton Park after losing the toss to host it. I got two goals to beat Bath 2–1, which put us through to the final. It is great to get to a cup final, no matter what level it's at, and we couldn't wait to get another cup for the Huish faithful, but things were taken out of our hands. It appeared we played an ineligible player in one of the early rounds, so the Somerset FA decided that we were to play Bath City again, the following May. The match became impossible for both teams to play due to contractual problems, so in the end, both us and Bath were thrown out of the competition and replaced by Clevedon Town, who were given the cup, it was a total farce for both teams.

As predicted, Wycombe Wanderers won the league, finishing top with 101 points. We again finished second with 92 points. It was so frustrating to be a runner up again, and it really made the lads determined that it was going to be third time lucky the following season. We knew Brian was going to give it everything and we as players were determined to do the same. I finished the campaign with 19 goals in 39 appearances, which made me top scorer. But I promised myself I would better it the following season, and boy did I do that.

Chapter Sixteen

The Cup & Me

The season of 1987–88 brought many changes for me. Not only had I become a dad for the first time, as Fil gave birth to our son Mark in the May, but working for Norm now as a labourer, along with running and exercising through the summer, had meant I'd shed a stone and a half pre-season. I never felt or looked fitter. The local press loved the story of my weight loss. I played up to it, having my photo taken, spade in hand, next to a cement mixer, with the headline: '*Slim Line Randall Looks The Part Again*'.

Yeovil had sorted out a new contract for me in the summer. It had gone up by about £30 to £150, which was still a decent wage for a part-time footballer. Particularly one with a new baby to look after. Brian Hall took us to Exeter University for the week with a fitness coach and we all benefited from the running and track work, even if we did all feel like throwing up after. Even John McGinley did what he was told. That week just showed how professional and forward thinking Brian was in those days. Off the field, the board had signed a contract to secure land at Hounstone for a new ground; selling the old Huish ground to supermarket chain Tesco in the process. So, the Glovers would have a brand new stadium in a few years. Everything was on the up for the club.

Hall made a few changes during the summer, bringing in former Chelsea keeper Bob Isles and Jeff Sherwood from Bath City. He also sold Carl Zachhau to Bishop's Stortford for around £7,000. It was going to be a tough season for Brian as the fans were still not happy with the fact that promotion was not achieved. Brian also had a very abrasive style when dealing with press and supporters, which meant they never really took to him.

As a coach, you couldn't fault him or his methods. We returned from our Exeter training camp, raring to go, showing our potential in a pre-season friendly against third division Gillingham and beating them 3–1. I was on fire, getting two of our goals, which were even more pleasing as my old Rovers team-mate Phil Kite was in the Gillingham goal. He joked that he didn't recognise me due to the weight loss. Losing the weight made a massive difference to my game; I felt quicker and couldn't wait for the season to start.

We kicked off the season with a 2–1 win away at Barking then continued winning our next games against Wokingham Town and Leytonstone. The Leytonstone win did our confidence the world of good as, pre-season, they were the bookies' favourites to win the league. We outplayed them in our 2–1 win. I got one of the goals and to be honest, I could have had a hat-trick. Our first defeat came against Basingstoke at the start of September as we went down 1–0 away from home, although we had wins in the FA Cup preliminary round and the AC Delco Cup. Further league defeats against Bromley and Bognor Regis meant that Hall's relationship with the fans was getting more and more strained. The defeat at Bognor always stays in my mind as I remember, before we kicked off, midfielder Ricky Chandler came up to me and said; 'Punky, I need a piss'.

'Fuck off, Rick, we're about to kick off', I replied.

'Honestly, I'm desperate', he said, jumping up and down like a little kid.

'Okay', I shouted, 'let's have a group huddle'.

So we all got round Ricky and he relieved himself in the middle of us. Unfortunately for Ricky, some supporters saw him and complained, which got Ricky a fine by the FA for his lewd behaviour.

In October, Hall decided to give up his job in the police force and go full-time with Yeovil. It was a brave decision by him and the board and it showed his commitment to getting it right at Huish Park. We ended the year still in contention at the top of the league, and also found ourselves in the first round of my beloved FA Cup, beating Gosport Borough, Waterlooville, Wimbourne, and Weymouth. Our first-round opponents were to be Worcester City, who we dispatched 1–0 after a replay, John McGinley getting our winner at Huish. That set us up with a round two appointment with Fourth Division Cambridge United. Okay, it wasn't a big draw for us but it was still league opposition. We really felt like we could put them to the sword.

The tie against Cambridge United had captured the Huish Faithful's imagination as around 1,000 supporters travelled up to watch the game. Everything about our preparation was first class. Brian was meticulous with preparation, so we had a good hotel the night before. Before the match, the board had told us that they would be giving us a bonus for winning the tie, which gave us even more impetus to win. Then midfielder Gary Donnellan told us all that he had just been in the bookies and we were 7/4 to win, so we all put a few quid on ourselves to win. Off we went to the match, with me and John McGinley stopping at the nearest off licence to get some beers for the way home, we were that confident. The game was a real battle, with both sides not giving much away, but Andy Wallace broke the deadlock for us and we ran out 1–0 winners, giving Yeovil their first league scalp in 15 years.

It was great for me, as I had a good game and I really felt that I could still do it in the Football League, although I did give a ball away late on, only to be saved by Geoff Sherwood, who made a fantastic tackle to save my blushes. The coach journey home was fantastic; we were all counting our winnings, especially me and John who had decided to charge for the beers we had bought. I came home with money stuffed in every pocket. Monday morning saw the cup draw and I listened to it on the radio while sat having my lunch on one of Norman's building sites. Yeovil came out first, then out popped QPR at home. I couldn't believe it, drawing a top side was all we could ask for. At training on the Tuesday night, everybody was buzzing about the news. The local press went to town on it, as did all the fans in and around the town.

The game was played in January. I had not really had that much success in front of goal towards the end of the year; in fact, I think I had only got five goals, which was really disappointing considering the start I had. But Huish Park was incredible that January afternoon. 10,000 were packed in. It was a fantastic atmosphere. The club had paraded out the few remaining players from the side that had beaten Sunderland all those year ago. The whole day reminded me of that afternoon against Southampton at Eastville. I loved the FA Cup and it will always have a special place in my heart. To add to the drama, the match was shown on the local HTV channel. People got a real sense that an upset was on the cards. The game was a real blood and guts affair, just what the third round of the FA Cup was all about. QPR boasted a really good side with players like Mark Falco, Paul Parker, Kevin Brock and Mark Dennis in the team and manager Trevor Francis had guided them to fifth in the First

Division. And here they were, facing labourers, policemen and forklift truck drivers. That's what the cup was all about.

The pitch was terrible, and not only for the slope. It looked like a ploughed field and the driving rain didn't help either. At least had we thought it would be a leveller. Although we gave a good account of ourselves, the giant killing never happened. We went down 3–0, although at 1–0 down I had a great chance. I was put through, one on one with the 'keeper. It was a chance that I could put away without looking – it was my trademark – but on that January afternoon, the ball rolled the wrong side of the post. The lads and me couldn't help but think what would have happened if I had made it 1–1. In fact, at training on the Tuesday after the game, we set up the same situation and I put the ball away 10 out of 10, which shows it just wasn't meant to be.

The game against QPR had earned the club £10,000, which was fantastic. Brian Hall made good use of the money he was given by the board, getting Steve Tapley from Enfield and bringing back former player Mick Docherty from Maidstone United. Hall also let Ricky Chandler go to Bath City in a swap deal with Martyn Grimshaw. He also sold Neil Coates to Dorchester Town. So with the club laying a lowly tenth in the league but with five games in hand on the leaders, we prepared ourselves for a big push for the title. We went on an unbeaten run and I hit a purple patch in front of goal, getting ten goals in the next six games as we charged up the table and did well in the AC Delco Cup, reaching the semi-finals. Suddenly, out of the blue Brian Hall called me to his office and told me that Cardiff City had been in touch. Their manager Frank Burrows wanted to speak to me about a possible move. I couldn't believe it; maybe I was going back to the Football League and at Cardiff City – the club that I always seemed to score against, and where I made my debut. Brian Hall said if they made an offer, Yeovil would not stand in my way. I told dad and he was thrilled for me as he still felt I could do it in the league. Fil also said that if I got the chance to go professional again then I should take it.

I arranged to meet Frank Burrows at Easton in Gordano service station, just outside Bristol, in the evening. I drove to the meeting and was surprisingly nervous. I think, deep down, I wanted this to happen as maybe I felt that I had one more shot in the league left in me. After all, I still could not believe no league club came in for me when I left Bristol Rovers.

I sat down with Frank and he asked me how I was. He also asked me if I thought I could still do it at league level, to which I said yes. He explained that Cardiff were at the top of the Fourth Division and pushing for promotion, and they needed some extra fire power in their bid to go up. The meeting went well. We shook hands and left it at that. But nothing happened; I never heard from Cardiff and neither did Yeovil. When I look back, I think that's when it hit me that maybe I was never going to get back into league football. I was disappointed but I thought, well, I have a job and I play for a good club at a high standard; perhaps it's not meant to be. Brian Hall said he was surprised they had not contacted the club but he was pleased I was staying, which was nice of him. So at least I could put it behind me and concentrate on getting the Glovers promotion.

I got two goals in the AC Delco Cup semi-final first leg, as we beat Kingstonian 2–0 at a packed Huish. We then beat them again at their place, 1–0 to get to the final against Hayes. We had climbed the league and were fighting it out with Bromley and Slough Town. When we beat Bromley 3–0 at our place, promotion looked a nailed-on certainty. Promotion was secured away at Tooting and Mitcham. I got the goals in a 2–1 win. To win the league was fantastic. We knew what it meant to the supporters. The club were on the up and the winners medal made up for my disappointment over the Cardiff transfer. With one medal on the shelf, I wanted another as we prepared to do the non-league double by winning the AC Delco Cup.

The match was at Basingstoke's ground. Our opponents, Hayes, had finished sixth in the league so we were favourites. The crowd was crammed into Basingstoke's ground, especially the Yeovil faithful who were packed behind the goal. The match was a tight affair but we came out winners, 3–1. I remember when I scored our second goal, the wall behind the goal collapsed as the Yeovil fans celebrated. The game was stopped as we helped the supporters up, but thankfully nobody was injured. We lifted the cup and paraded it in front of the supporters. It could have been the FA Cup for all I cared, it meant just as much to me. We had now won the cup as well as promotion to the conference. The supporters had still not really taken to manager Brian Hall, even though he had set out what he wanted to do from the start, which was to get this club nearer the football league. I even started to think that maybe I would get there after all with Yeovil. I had scored 25 goals that season and amazingly, I had played in 65 matches, which is incredible.

Brian Hall wasted no time in making changes for our appearance in the conference. Surprisingly, he let John McGinley leave the club. He never really saw eye to eye with John. I don't really think Brian rated him as a player, which was laughable when you consider John went on to play in the Premier League with Bolton Wanderers and gained two Scottish caps later in his career. Off the field, season ticket sales had gone through the roof and well over 3,000 saw our first game in the conference, a 1–1 draw with Wycombe Wanderers. I got off the mark in our second game, a 2–2 draw away at Kidderminster Harriers. It is always nice to get off the mark early in the season, especially when you are playing at a higher level. We lifted another trophy in August; the Vauxhall Charity Shield, beating last year's rivals Bromley 4–1, with Mick Docherty grabbing a hat-trick. With John McGinley gone, Hall realised that maybe we were a bit thin on the ground in terms of strikers and he dipped into the loan market. There were all sorts of rumours over who was coming. I couldn't believe it when, one night at training, I heard a familiar Scouse accent say; 'fuck me, Punky, I won't have to do any painting here will I?'

They had got Archie Stephens on loan from Carlisle United.

'Christ, Archie,' I said, 'you couldn't have got any further from Carlisle'.

Archie was in and out of the side at Carlisle and just came down for a couple of weeks. I know Yeovil wanted to make it a permanent transfer but Archie was settled up north with his family. We held our own in the division and come the end of the year, we found ourselves in the first round of the FA Cup again, this time beating Merthyr Tydfil 3–2 in front of 4,000 supporters at Huish. That put us in the next round, where our opponents were to be another league outfit, Torquay United. Again, the FA Cup captured the imagination of the Yeovil public; they really got behind the team as we lined up in front of over 5,000 fans at Huish Park.

It was the seasiders who struck first, when they sprung our offside trap, fifteen minutes in. We battled back with the crowd behind us and, on half an hour, the ball came to me. With my back to goal, I flicked the ball up over the Torquay defender and swivelled to volley the ball into the net, putting us level. Looking back, it was one of the best goals I have ever scored and to get it in the cup match was a bit special. I ran to the Yeovil fans, who were going berserk all around the ground. It felt like it was the Southampton game all over again. Torquay were there for the taking and later in the game, I had a further two chances that I should have put away, but in the end they hung out for a draw. As with most of the smaller sides in the FA Cup, it appears they get just one chance, and that happened to us as we lost the replay at Plainmoor 1-0. We were disappointed but the directors made a few quid out of the run, although there were to be no bonuses this time.

Brian Hall was feeling the pressure with the fans on his back, especially now the cup run was over. He made some changes, moving my mate Dave Linney to Basingstoke and also bringing in a soldier from Waterlooville called Guy Whittingham who would go on to play at the very top with Portsmouth and Aston Villa. Guy was a very gifted lad, a bit raw at the time but you could still see that he was a bit special, as he got four goals in his first four games. I enjoyed playing upfront with him. Tony Ricketts also left for Bath City in a deal worth £10,000. After a couple of heavy defeats, the supporters would get on our backs, which they were entitled to do. After one game, I was walking to my car with my kit bag when one came up to me and started screaming; 'you're fucking shit Randall, you're bloody useless, you bastard'. He then came towards me and I honestly thought he was going to hit me, so I dropped my bag and got myself ready but off he went, still shouting abuse at me. This was a one off, as on the whole, the Yeovil fans were very good to me. They had just got promotion and they wanted it again, which, to be honest, was unrealistic.

My last game in the green and white of Yeovil was against Paulton Rovers at home in the Somerset Premier Cup. I got one in a 9–0 thrashing of our West Country neighbours. It was just after Christmas when I got a call from Brian Hall, who told me that Bath City had made a cheeky bid for me and the Yeovil board had agreed. I was dumbfounded; I couldn't believe they had said yes, but looking back they must have thought that they had a perfect replacement in Guy Whittingham. I met Bath City's manager, Jeff Evans, and he was so excited to get me. He said they needed a striker and took a gamble on asking Yeovil. In truth, Jeff could not believe they had said yes. I had no hesitation in going to Yeovil's rivals. All I wanted was to keep playing, and that was now going to be at Twerton Park. I had scored 12 goals in 38 games, including reserve games, in my last season at Huish Park. I am extremely proud to have pulled on the Yeovil shirt and to have been a part of their terrific history. To see them now, in that new stadium and in the football league, makes me feel very proud to have played for them. I only wish I could have got to the football league with them. There are some great people at the club and even today, the fans give me a wonderful reception and I'm very honoured by that. So here I was, 31 years old and facing another challenge: not only to keep scoring, but to win over the Bath City fans.

Chapter Seventeen

Record Breaker

I had no trouble joining Yeovil Town's rivals, Bath City. Like most players throughout the game, I just wanted to play where I was wanted. Unfortunately for me that was no longer at Huish Park. After speaking to Bath manager Jeff Evans, it was clear that Bath were very keen to get my signature.

I signed at Bath's ground, Twerton Park, for about £160 per week plus bonuses, which I was more than happy with. It was a two-year deal. The move coincided with a change of job for me. I stopped working for Norm and started working as a barman at Tor Leisure in Glastonbury. It was a club-come-bar and I was offered the job through a friend. The job entailed sorting out deliveries, setting the pumps up and obviously working with the public. After spending so much of my spare time at Stoke in bars, I obviously thought I was well qualified to stand the other side of the bar. Norm was great about me leaving, especially as the new job would fit better with my footballing schedule. I would work nine 'till three or six 'till 11, and if I had a game I could have the time off, no problem.

Bath City, like Yeovil, had a big non-league reputation; they were giant-killers in their day and had a great footballing history, producing great players like ex-Manchester City captain Tony Book, and Charlie Fleming who had played for Sunderland in the 1950s as well as the great Stan Mortensen who again played for Blackpool in the 50s. They were currently in the Southern Premier League and like many teams in that league, had ambitions to get to the conference and then the football league. Ironically, they were sharing their Twerton Park ground with Bristol Rovers, who had left Eastville and moved to Bath until they could find another site in Bristol for a new stadium. Jeff Evans had only just taken over and the club, which was lying mid-table with only a few games left of the season.

Walking into that Bath City dressing room for the first time had a real effect on me. I felt immediately at home, just like when I signed for Rovers as a young man. The atmosphere was great. I arrived with a bit of a reputation but it meant nothing to the lads as they took to me right away. A lot of the players at Bath at that time had been with league clubs; people like Gary Smart, Dave Palmer and Keith Brown, who had all been at Bristol Rovers. Dave Payne and Ricky Chandler had tasted league football with Bristol City, and Tony Ricketts had been at Yeovil with me. It made for a decent side. I think part of the great team spirit at that time was the fact that everybody was local. I had been in the dressing room at Yeovil, where it was a split between London lads and local, and we never gelled as a unit; we just became two camps. After all, it's difficult to go out socially with teammates when they live the other side of London and you're in Somerset. But at Bath it was the perfect mix. I made my debut at home against Ashford Town. I was up front with a lad called John Freeguard, who I would strike up a great partnership with in my time there. John was a big target man and we complemented each other well. He was a local lad and had great touch. I found it hard to believe that he had not been spotted over the years and given his chance in the Football League, but that's football, as I knew too well.

I got a great reception from the Bath fans and that pleased me, considering my Yeovil connections. I had been a bit of a thorn in the side of Bath supporters over the years, with my goals against them, but they seemed to forget that, especially when we ran out 4–0 winners and I got two of the goals. To score on my debut in front of the Bath fans was fantastic; the feeling of elation when that ball hits the net is something that never goes away, even to this day. It doesn't matter if you are Wayne Rooney, transferred for 100 million, or Fred Smith playing for the Dog and Duck, if you're a striker you are always judged on goals and that first one you get for a new club is a great feeling. It lifts the pressure of you, no matter who you are. I am sure the Bath fans took to me because of the goals and also with Bristol Rovers ground sharing with Bath City. A lot of Rovers fans would go and see Bath as a sort of second club.

My relationship with the Twerton faithful grew as I got another two goals in my next game, when we dispatched Burton Albion 5–1 at home. I was really happy with my start, as was the manager, but after the Burton game he came to see me and told me that he had bad news. My mind was racing ahead, thinking what it could be. He shuffled about from foot to foot and said; 'Paul, your cup tied for the Somerset cup semi-final against Mangotsfield United on Tuesday'. I was disappointed, as Mangotsfield were managed by my old Rovers reserve boss, Harold Jarman. Jeff then asked if I would turn out for the Bath Reserves against Backwell. I laughed and said; 'Of course I will'. Jeff told me a few years ago that he was nervous about asking me, as he did not know if I would be pre-pared to play on a Tuesday night in front of about 20 people, in a reserve team game surrounded by kids. I did not care, as all I wanted to do was play football and being with the young lads, I thought if I could help a few it would be great.

I was never the big-time Charlie and enjoyed the game, even if it was bloody freezing if I remember rightly.

The season ended with Bath in mid-table. My own scoring record was six goals in six games, which meant I could not wait for a full season at the club. It was just at the start of the new campaign when I got the news that Jeff Evans had left the club to be assistant at Frome Town. I was shocked, as I really liked Jeff; after all, he was the man who brought me to the club. Although a lot of the players were worried about who was going to take over, I had seen it all before and just got on with my own game.

I think the board just wanted a change and Jeff was just unlucky. His replace-ment was to be George Rooney. George was a scouser so I immediately thought I had a chance with him. He had experience managing Worcester City where he had done a great job and also Altrincham, where again he had been suc-cessful. His first job was to bring in Chris Banks, a 24-year-old defender from Port Vale. Banksy was class and could have easily played League Football, but he chose to join us at Bath which was a real coup by George. Banksy later went on to play for Cheltenham Town. He also promoted youngster Rob Cousins into the first team squad from the youth team. We played a couple of pre-sea-son friendlies; the first one being against Southampton. I remember the game well, it was a lovely sunny day and there was a good crowd at Twerton Park. I remember getting kicked to pieces by a young 17-year-old in the Southampton defence. He had legs like tree trunks and even though he was a youngster, I remember thinking; 'who the fuck is this?' After the game, we had a chat and he told me he was on the verge of the first team. I wished him all the best for the season. His name? Neil Ruddock.

We lost the game 3–1; I scored our only goal from the penalty spot. I never ever took penalties but on this occasion I was nearest the ball and nobody wanted to take it, so I stepped up and hit it into the net. We had played well and against top opposition so that gave us a lot of heart for our next friendly against tenants Bristol Rovers – a game I couldn't wait to play in. I got a great reception from the Rovers fans as I always did. It was a weird situation really, as we both shared the same ground while they looked for a home of their own in Bristol. This was a logistical nightmare for poor old kit man Ray Kendall, who told me that on match days, not only did he have to get the kit from the training ground at Hambrook, but then he had to drive it to Bath – about 20 miles away. Then he would take down all the Bath City pictures in the boardroom and replace them with Bristol Rovers pictures. After the game, he would do it all again. Fair play to Kendo, he was Rovers through and through.

Gerry Francis managed Rovers at the time and it was to be the start of a great season for the club as they won the league, gaining promotion to the Second Division. The title was that much sweeter as they pipped neighbours City, who finished second. They had a decent side, with Ian Holloway the main man in midfield. On that afternoon they beat us 3–0. I did not get much of a kick as I was marked by Geoff Twentyman and Billy Clark, both players who would be a rock in the defence for the Gas that season.

We continued with a couple of friendlies against local non-league sides and although I was pleased with my game, I only hit the net once, which was in a 4–0 win against Fairford Town. We opened our Southern League campaign against Cambridge City, losing away 2–1. All the lads were gutted; we had not played that well and George Rooney certainly told us in no uncertain terms that we had not performed. The words from George certainly worked, as we went the next eight games unbeaten. My tally now stood at eight goals. I was working really well with John Freeguard up front. We also had Gary Smart who played wide left, and I worked well with him. I don't know if it was age, but I felt much more relaxed at Bath City. I thought I was going to score in every game. We lost our unbeaten run away at Waterlooville, losing 1–0, but it did not dent our confidence. We rose up the table after going on a 12-game unbeaten run, which saw me get another eight goals. We were now going neck and neck with Dover Athletic at the top of the table. We had a great team spirit at the club. Most of the lads enjoyed a drink with the fans after home games and I think we all bonded as a unit; players and fans alike. End of the year, we drew Fulham in the first round of the FA Cup. Everybody at the club was ecstatic. Fulham, at the time, were a Third Division side but it did not bother us as it was still a league side, and that's all us and the fans wanted from the draw.

I again was featured heavily in the build-up by the press and I loved it as usual. I always seemed to have a good relationship with the local press and would always pose for whatever picture they wanted. This time it was me and Filomena pushing the kids on swings at the park and the article was talking about the new and relaxed family man, Paul Randall, who could cause an FA Cup upset. It was nice also that Fulham boss Ray Lewington came out in the press and said that I was the marksman they had to watch. A crowd of 5,000 packed into Twerton, to hopefully see a giant-killing act. The match was toe to toe in the first half, and we went in at the break 0–0. George told us to keep plugging away and something would happen for us. Fulham were a good side, with players like Clive Walker, Jeff Eckhard and Gary Bennett. Within two minutes of the restart, a long throw fell to Freeguard and as quick as lightning he swivelled 180 degrees and whipped the ball into the net to put us 1–0 up. We jumped all over him and the crowd went wild. Minutes later, Dave Palmer hoisted the ball to the far post. I knew Freeguard would go up for it, so I drifted into the six-yard box, waiting for a knock down. Sure enough, he headed it and the ball came off their keeper and fell to me to tap it in and put us 2–0 up. It was a wonderful feeling; here I was in my thirties, getting a goal in the FA Cup again. Unfortunately for us, they battled back and made it 2–2 in the dying minutes. I don't know if it was a combination of lack of fitness against full-timers, or lack of experience. We wanted three instead of killing the game but the directors were happy with another payday at Craven Cottage. The supporters were brilliant to us, even though we felt like we had lost. As for me, I was pleased to be going to Craven Cottage again; a ground where I had done well over the years.

As it turned out, the game at Twerton Park was our one chance to beat Fulham. We lost the replay 2–1, with Gary Smart getting our goal. In the two games we felt that we had not let the supporters down. The cup defeat never affected our form in the league, as we embarked on a 12-game unbeaten run, which included a 1–0 win at home to rivals Dover at the end of the year. Again, my partnership with John Freeguard was on fire, and we ended the year with my tally at 25 and John's at 19. It was incredible. Our run continued with George getting the Manager of the Month award for both January and February, but Dover were matching us stride for stride in the chase for the title. Although John and myself were getting all the local media attention, Gary Smart and Chris Banks in particular, along with all the lads, were having a great season.

Supporters were also telling me of John Fairbrother's record 44 goals in the 1974–75 season, and how they thought I could break it. I was flattered but my only thoughts were on turning over Dover at the top of the league.

Our form continued as we put teams to the sword. Our only problem was that Dover were doing exactly the same, matching us result for result. As we entered the month of March, I was, unbelievably, three goals away from Fairbrother's record. At Alvechurch I scored a hat trick in a 5–0 win to equal it. I was honoured to have equalled such a long record – 44 goals in a season is a tremendous feat at any level. With it, came paper talk of a move back to Rovers. Apparently manager Gerry Francis had expressed an interest in taking me as cover for his young strikers, as they also were involved in a promotion race. I heard nothing officially or from Bath City, but the papers were full of it. I must admit, if I had been offered the chance I would have ripped their hand off. The chance to pull on that blue and white quarter shirt one last time, even if it was for 10 minutes, would have been too much to turn down. I was happy at Bath City, my home life was great and I was enjoying the bar work, but as I said, the chance to go back to Rovers would have been too much of a pull for me.

The press loved the fact that I had broken the record and they put me in touch with Trevor Tiley and his two sons, Richard and Adam. Trevor was a greeting card wholesaler, and he and his sons were huge Bath City fans. At the start of the season, the boys had sponsored me £1 a goal each, so the story was about how much I was costing their dad. We had our photos taken with each other at the ground and had a bit of a laugh. Meeting them was something I will never forget. I loved stuff like that, meeting the fans and having a laugh with them, I think the atmosphere around the club at that time was the key to our season.

I broke the record home to Ashford in a 4–0 win. I was ecstatic; after all, that's what a goal-scorer is judged on, and to beat any scoring record is great.

As we tried desperately to take the title with five games to go, Gary Smart broke his leg in a 3–3 draw with Weymouth. It was during a challenge from Mickey Tanner, an old teammate of mine from Yeovil. There was a lot of bad feeling about it from the lads but I don't think Mickey did it on purpose, even though it was awful. We were all gutted for Smarty but we thought, right, let's win this for him. We then went onto win all five remaining games, but it was not enough as Dover took the league with 102 points, and we finished second with 98. I had scored an incredible 51 goals to smash the record. I feel it's a record that will not be broken for a very long time, if ever. Losing the league was gutting but to have the record at least gave me something to remember the season by.

Or so I thought. Later that month, myself and all the players received phone calls from George Rooney to tell us that the Dover pitch and facilities were not up to FA rules so we would be going into the conference instead. I felt sorry for the Dover lads, who had done so well that season, but here I was, 32 years old and going back to the conference. It was tremendous and I could not wait for the new season to start.

Chapter Eighteen

Returning Home

Everyone at Twerton was on a high during the summer months. To be back in the conference was fantastic for Bath City. Although we may have got there by default, we were determined to show everyone that we could hold our own in the division. George told us that staying in the league was our priority. It was going to be a tough season, but we looked forward to the challenge ahead.

Dad had been busy in the summer, getting the Glastonbury assistant manager's job. This would mean he would not be able to come and see all my games. This news did not bother me, as I was thrilled he was at the club and doing a job I thought he was born to do. I think he would have made a great football manager and Glastonbury was made for him. George got busy in the summer bringing in local lad Paul Hirons. Paul had played at Bristol Rovers as a youngster and had now been released by Torquay United. George also brought Paul's teammate Ian Weston to the club, along with centre-half Richard Crowley, who came from Cheltenham Town. We had lost Smarty for the whole of the coming season but George had kept the nucleus of last season's squad to help us stay up in this league. This meant me and John Freeguard were up front again to start where we left off last campaign. I had scored 51 goals that season and John had got 36 so everyone was keen to see what we could do in the higher division.

We played a couple of friendlies against Bristol Rovers in the lead up to the new season, and also a game against Mangotsfield, who were now managed by my old mate Harold Jarman. It was great to see him and reminisce about the old days at Rovers. Our first league game was home to Kettering Town and we found ourselves 3–0 up at half-time, with goals from Freeguard, Chris Smith and myself. I always say it's great to get off the mark as early as possible as a striker so to get one in the first game of the season was a relief. In the second half, we collapsed as Kettering came back and scored three goals to earn a 3–3 draw. George ripped into every one of us and told us that if we played like we did in the second half we would go straight down. I picked up an injury that forced me to miss the next couple of games. We struggled in them, getting only two goals in nine matches. George then dipped into the transfer market, signing Mickey Tanner from Weymouth. The lads were surprised and so were the supporters; after all, it was only a couple of months since he was involved in the challenge that broke Gary Smart's leg. But we welcomed him into the side.

We were struggling and couldn't seem to find a win from anywhere. Off the field, things got worse for the club. I was listening to the radio before I went to work, when I heard that the main stand at Twerton Park had burnt down in the night. It was just days before Bristol Rovers were due to play Bristol City; some people from the social club at Bath had noticed smoke and raised the alarm. The stand was saved but the damage was going to cost a fortune. Bath and Rovers supporters got together and got it to a state where it could be used within a week, so a temporary stand was put in place. It was a massive blow for both clubs but credit to everybody involved, who all rallied round. Nine Bristol City supporters were arrested and charged with arson. The incident just served to increase the animosity that both Bristol clubs had for each other at that time.

George dipped into the transfer market again to try and lift our fortunes, bringing in Adie Mings from Chippenham. Adie was a strong, powerful lad who played upfront. He also brought another striker, Nigel Hawkins, in on loan from Blackpool, but Nigel only lasted a couple of games as he broke his jaw in a game at Wycombe Wanderers and went back to his parent club up north. The dressing room had become very different, with long-term injuries to Dave Palmer and Paul Stevens. George had also let Mickey Tanner leave as fast as he had joined, and Paul Hirons also left to go to Yeovil. We were at the bottom of the league but the board still backed George. He again brought in players like Jerry Gill in defence along with Sean Lundon, a striker from Chester City. Mickey Mellon also came on loan from Bristol City, but poor old Mickey broke his leg at Yeovil on New Year's Day. It had been a bad day all round at Huish, not only had I got unbelievable abuse from the crowd – which, when I think back, I was always going to get now I was playing for their rivals – but we lost 3–2 as well.

Surprisingly, George sold John Freeguard and Chris Smith to Gloucester City as he tried to change the squad. I was gutted, as both of them had been the main men in our promotion year. I started to think that maybe George was running out of ideas and in February, the board had enough and George was sacked, with Bath City lying at the bottom of the table. I thought the new manager was certainly going to have a job on his hands here, whoever he was. The Bath directors wasted no time and installed centre-half Tony Ricketts in temporary charge till the end of the season. I think they just wanted to see if Ricko could keep us up. Tony had played with me at Yeovil; he was a good bloke but at times we didn't always see eye to eye. But now he was my boss and I wanted the same as he did, which was to keep Bath City in the conference.

Tony put me up front with Adie Mings. It went well as Adie was quick like me, but about fifteen years younger, so I did all the thinking and he did all the running. We got a win at last; beating Cheltenham 2–0. Adie and I got the goals. We then put a bit of a run together, losing only twice in nine games, to keep us up by three points. We knew we had not had the greatest season but we stayed in the conference and I had got 22 goals.

Work started in earnest on the main stand at Twerton, which was a fantastic achievement by the club. The financial responsibility weighed heavily on the directors. The board installed Tony Ricketts as manager and gave him a two-year deal. Some of the supporters felt that Ricko was a cheap option but to be fair to him, he had kept us up when all seemed lost and if he was cheap then it just reflected the tough financial constraints the club was experiencing. The club had lost £30,000 the previous year and I know that doesn't seem a lot by today's standards, but for a non-league side, any loss was a problem. Many people at the time expressed a worry as to what might happen if Bristol Rovers did eventually move out and take their rent money with them. The board, to their credit, backed Ricko in the transfer market as he tried to wheel and deal. He knew he was up against it, as did the bookies, making us favourites for relegation. Ricko immediately brought some experience to the side in the form of my old Rovers teammate Peter Aitken. Pete could still play but he also took the reserves and passed on the vast knowledge of the game he had. The previous season had seen Mangotsfield United's front two, Andy Perrett and Martyn Boyle, score over 100 goals between them in what had been an astonishing season for the club. Ricko signed them both, which shocked me a bit as nothing was said to me regarding my own place in the side, but I had been around long enough to know that competion for places could only help a club. I just got my head down and made sure that the Bath supporters would see nothing but 100% from me as usual.

I was picked in the first game of the campaign, partnering Martyn Boyle up front as we beat Northwich Victoria 3–1 away. I managed to get two, which was a great start for me and also sent a bit of a message out that I could still do it. I was pleased for Ricko; he got his first win of the season and it lifted some of the pressure off him. All the lads were in great spirits after our first win, and it was also great to see Gary Smart return to training after his time out with a broken leg.

Our optimism was short lived, as we couldn't find a win in our next five league games. Although we were mid-table, the supporters were not happy as they saw the type of football we were playing as route-one stuff. I never had a problem with how we played, as my game was always running on to through balls, even at 35 years old. But after my spell at Stoke City, I had become more accomplished at keeping the ball and holding it up to get midfielders involved in the play. I was still scoring and by the end of the year had got 17 goals, which, considering my age and the youngsters after my shirt, I was more than happy with. The supporters were not a happy bunch as we constantly seemed to struggle at home, which understandably frustrated them and us. Ricko did not help his cause when Chris Townsend was transferred to Gloucester City on a free transfer; months after Ricko paid £12,000 for him. The supporters knew the club was strapped for cash and they could not believe the club could lose that sort of money, especially when they were fundraising for the club at every opportunity. The financial situation also meant the board announced that the reserves would be disbanding at the end of the season as a cost-saving exercise. Looking back, it seemed so short-sighted. Where were the future Bath City players going to learn the game? Typical of the sort of man Peter Aitken is, he resigned and told the club that it wouldn't be right for him to still take a wage now the reserves were going. That's Peter to a tee; an honest, top bloke. I'm sure many would have gone on drawing their money but not Peter – I think he had genuine affection for the club and I was sad to see him go. And I'm glad to see him working now as the community officer at Bristol Rovers. He is truly one of the game's good blokes.

We were knocked out of the FA Cup 2–1 by Worcester City, so there was also no chance of a cup run, which could have made the board a few quid. So it became imperative for us to stay in the conference, as relegation would be a disaster for the club. We entered the New Year with two draws against Wycombe Wanderers and Yeovil Town. Yeovil were playing at their new stadium which had been open for a year; it was still called Huish Park but it was a fantastic facility that just showed you what could be achieved if football clubs, the private sector and local councils all got together to make something happen. I couldn't help think of Bristol Rovers, who were still waiting for a ground in Bristol. But fair play to the Yeovil board, they made that dream come true.

The New Year also saw me score my 100th goal for Bath City in the 5–0 drubbing of Welling. I was really pleased to have reached the milestone, particularly as now I was appearing more on the bench. I just had a feeling that I may not be in Ricko's plans. The season came to an end with us losing 2–0 away at Stafford Rangers. Ricko had done a good job in very difficult circumstances and we finished ninth in the league, which was fantastic. I again finished the season as the leading goal-scorer at the club, with 26 goals in all matches. I felt that I had done my job even though I was now approaching my 36th birthday. The 1992–93 season would, unbeknown to me, turn out to be my last season at Bath City. It's very sad when I look back. That season had some memorable moments for me. I think I knew the writing was on the wall the season before, when Ricko would tell me where to stand at corners. I would always, throughout my career, stand in the six yard box, right next to the keeper in case of any knock-downs or flick-ons, but Ricko insisted I stand outside the box and run in late. It sounds trivial but it annoyed me; after all, I was still scoring goals, and I never told him how to defend a corner. I know he was the boss but at 35 years of age, did I really need advice on where to stand at a corner? I said earlier in this book that Ricko and I never saw eye to eye. Although he was a good bloke and did well for Bath City, I always felt there was something of an atmosphere between us.

One of the great memories for me at Bath City was in my last season, when we drew Glastonbury Town away in the FA Cup first qualifying round. I could not believe it. To go back to the club where it had all started for me was magical, and with my dad as assistant manager, the game turned out to be a wonderful occasion. I knew most of the Glastonbury lads; this was where I had done nearly all my pre-season work throughout my career. A packed crowd gave me the most fantastic reception as I ran out. The feeling was one that still gives me goose bumps when I think of it today. We won the game 4–0 and I got two of the goals. I remember one of them was a chip from the edge of the box that went in over the 'keeper; even the Glastonbury crowd clapped it as a piece of audacious skill. Dad sat there, in the dugout next to manager Simon White, with his head in his hands. The bar afterwards was packed. I think the whole town wanted to buy me a drink. God knows what time I eventually got home to Fil and the kids. It was a great day all round.

Ricko was bringing in strikers, so I found myself on the bench again. It would be a lie to say it never bothered me; even at my age, I wanted to play. The supporters loved it when I did get in the team, and I think that was the dilemma Ricko had. He would I'm sure have let me go earlier in his time as manager, but I was still scoring, so in a way I felt a bit like he was stuck with me.

Being on the bench was frustrating, as I wanted to play all the time. One game in particular stuck in my mind as the beginning of the end for me at Bath. After beating Glastonbury in the early rounds of the FA Cup, we progressed to the proper first round, the round where the league teams joined. We drew Cardiff City at Ninian Park. I always had a good record against Cardiff and I was really up for the game, especially after my meeting with their manager Frank Burrows. I was desperate to play and show the Cardiff fans what I could do.

I was named sub for the game, with youngster Deion Vernon taking my place. Deion was a real talent, he had been released from Bristol City and had a real impact at Bath. He was the future of the club but I was sure at some point Ricko would put me on, even for five minutes. Bath won the game 3–2, with young Dion getting one of the goals, but I never got on, which really disappointed me. Although it was a fantastic giant-killing act, I never really felt part of it. The team took a lap of honour from the Cardiff and Bath fans and I just watched. Ricko obviously made the right decision as the team had won, but I had never felt so bitterly disappointed not to have got on. That's when I started to feel that maybe my time in the black and white shirt was coming to an end.

We drew Northampton in the next round at Twerton Park. Again I was named sub. I wondered if I would get on, as Twerton was buzzing with the expectations of another cup shock. 3,270 turned up for the match. All the lads were confident but Northampton was a different kettle of fish to Cardiff and they were 2–1 up with 10 minutes to go. I was desperate to get on when suddenly, Ricko told me to warm up because I was going on. I emerged onto the touchline and the crowd started to chant my name, which was fantastic. It showed I had not been forgotten by them. I came on for Deion and in the very last minute of the game, the ball fell to me. I hit this cross as hard as I could towards the box. I watched it in the air and it suddenly looped over the 'keeper and into the Northampton net to rescue the tie and give no time for Northampton to come back. The crowd went crazy. I just turned to them with my arms open and a big smile on my face as if to say; 'what about that then?' It was fantastic, almost like my final act for Bath City.

We lost the replay 3–0 a couple of days later, but people were still talking about the goal. I was in and out of the side and finished the season with seven goals. The club had another good season, finishing seventh in the league. At the end of the campaign, I got the call to Ricko's office, where he told me that he was letting me go. I shook his hand, wished him all the best and told him that I was still going on the end of season trip to Tenerife that all us lads had saved up for all year. And with that, I left the club. I walked into the car park and before I got in my car, I looked back at Twerton Park. I thought about the fabulous supporters and all the good times I had at the club. I was now 36 years of age and wondered if I should hang up those Randall boots. Not a chance. I wanted to play for as long as I could. With that, I drove back to Glastonbury and thought about where I would end up next.

Chapter Nineteen

Journeyman

The team had a great time in Tenerife. It was a bit of a last hurrah for those of us that Ricko had shown the door to; lads like me, Dave Mogg, Graham Withey and Dave Singleton. I was gutted to leave Bath City, I felt that I was worth at least another season at the club, and the bond we had as a team was so special that it was a real blow to have to walk away from.

I returned from Tenerife needing a holiday to recover from it, but Fil was never going to let that happen. I wasn't too worried about whether another club was going to come in for me. I had a decent reputation in front of goal and I just hoped whoever it was would be of a decent standard. Many people asked if I was going to hang my boots up but I always remembered my mate Ron Stoodley. Ron had broken his leg playing and gave up straight after. He was in his thirties and he told me he regretted it ever since and told me to play for as long as I could. I was still enjoying my football so when I got a call in the summer I was thrilled. The call was from Weymouth manager Bill Coldwell. Bill asked if he could come to my house and chat about me joining them. I was excited at the prospect. Bill was an ex-Weymouth player who had also worked at Birmingham City as a scout. He had also been caretaker manager on two occasions, when Dave Mackay left and when Lou Macari had left St Andrews. He arrived in the evening and he told me about his plans for the club. They were in the Southern League Premier Division. Bill had signed up a lot of young lads from Plymouth Argyle, Exeter City and Torquay United and he was also in the process of bringing ex-Reading goal-scorer Trevor Senior to the club. He wanted me and Trevor to play up front together and help the youngsters. Although I was excited about what he had to say, I was a bit put off by the travelling which would mean a round trip of 120 miles twice a week for training.

Bill told me he could pay me £120 a week plus £10 per goal and £10 per win. With the thoughts of the travelling involved still going round my head, I said I would let him know as he left. A few minutes later, the door rang and it was Bill. He said; 'look Paul, we really want to sign you so how about £20 a goal and £20 a win?' Bill obviously thought I was a tough negotiator, which I plainly wasn't, but I just liked the fact that he really wanted me to sign so we shook hands and I joined Weymouth on a year's contract.

Bill signed Trevor Senior. Trevor was a big centre-forward who had started his career at Farnborough Town and gained a reputation at Portsmouth and Middlesbrough, but it was at Reading where he found cult status with the fans due to his scoring record. We played well together. I think I got six goals in my first couple of games so the fans took to me straight away. But it just didn't feel right. The dressing room was so young; me and Trevor were like two dads in the squad. After matches I was used to going to the clubhouse bar chatting to the fans, but all the lads went home. After games it would be just me and Trevor sat there like two old codgers, putting the world to rights. The travelling was getting to me also. For away games, I had to drive up to Basingstoke and meet the team in the service station, as most of our games were in the London area. I remember coming back from one game in my Ford Escort when it blew up on Salisbury Plain. I had to walk miles to find the nearest house and get them to let me use their phone whilst not letting them think I was some escaped nutter. I phoned dad to tow me home and it was the last straw. After a couple of months, Clevedon Town said they were interested in signing me. It was nearer home so I told Bill I was leaving to join them. Bill was not pleased, and he did everything to make me stay. Looking back, they were a good club and very professional but it just never felt right at Weymouth. So I found myself on the move again.

Clevedon were another club with good facilities. They were owned by Barry Bradshaw, who was also a director of Bristol Rovers, and managed by Steve Fey. I met Steve and he said he would match what Weymouth were paying me. We shook hands and I signed until the end of the season. Clevedon were doing well and I found myself on the bench all the time. Again, after a few games I met with Steve and I said; 'I just want to get a game, Steve'. He agreed that I had not been given a chance due to him not wanting to change a winning side.

We agreed it was not my fault or his, but I felt it was best I left. I left Clevedon without even playing a full game. Again it was a case of a lovely club that was just was not right for me at that time.

Throughout this time I never felt like hanging up the boots. I just wanted to play football. I still enjoyed everything about the game. Unbeknown to me, Dad had given Welton Rovers a ring and informed them that I was available. I sat down with their manager, Alan O'Leary. He said he would pay me £75 a game. I joined and they were a good bunch of lads, some of whom had watched me from the terraces at Eastville in my Bristol Rovers days. I remember my debut for Welton against Barnstaple – we won 2–0 and I got one of the goals. It was a ball played over the top for me to run on to, which was bread and butter for me even though I was fast approaching 40. I put the ball away. Afterwards, the lads said the moment I ran onto it they knew it was going in the back of the net. I played a few games for Welton but then I was pulled to one side by manager Alan, who told me the club just couldn't pay me that sort of money anymore. They were in the Western League and had probably been over ambitious in what they paid me. Again it was a good club and I would have stayed but the next offer was too good to turn down.

Dad was assistant manager at Glastonbury Town and he asked me if I would be interested in signing for them. I was thrilled. The thought of going back and playing for the club that started my career seemed perfect. Dad arranged for manager Simon White to meet me at Tor Leisure and chat about what they had to offer. Simon asked me what money I was on at Welton. He told me he couldn't match it, but he could go to £50 a game. I asked him what the rest of the lads were on, and he said £20. 'I will have that then' I told him. So off I went and signed for the club of my youth.

I was going back to the club that I played for at 14 years old. And now, over half a century later, I would be pulling on a Glastonbury shirt again. We had a fantastic team with plenty of characters, in particular one called James Dash, or Dashy as he was known. Now Dashy wasn't your typical part-time footballer. He lived in a big house with its own grounds. We used to call him Lord Dashy and when we picked him up we used to rib him about what wing he slept in. I first met him in a pre-season game against Paulton Rovers. As far as he was concerned, I was just some bloke who had turned up hoping to get in the team. Everything went well for me; my touch was bang on. I scored in the game and Dashy said to one of the lads at the back; 'who's that bloke we got up front? He is ever so good.'

The lads fell about laughing; 'that's Paul Randall, you stupid twat'.

They told him I'd played for Bristol Rovers and Stoke City. That's what I liked about Dashy, he genuinely had no idea that I had played professionally.

Dad and Simon had created a really good atmosphere at the club. It was the first time that dad had managed me but in truth, he had been managing me all my career so having him shouting in training was nothing new. I was used to it, and I loved spending time with him. The club had obviously changed from my youth days. They played at a new ground called Abbey Moor Stadium, but a lot of the background staff and volunteers – the lifeblood of any non-league team at that level – were still at the club. They were genuinely pleased to see me back at the club, which was really special for me.

In my first season I scored around 25 goals as Glastonbury finished in the top half of the Western league. The following season, again I got around 25 goals, as we battled at the top of the league with Backwell United. We came through in the end and won promotion to the Western League Premier Division. Everyone at the club was delighted. It was great to share the experience with dad, and really special that we had done it together. But then our joy was turned to anger as we were told by the league that we could not go up as the ground did not meet with the league requirements. We were all shell-shocked as Backwell went up in our place. I now knew how those Dover Players had felt when it happened to them when I was at Bath City. We all had a meeting and we spoke to the owners of the club, but they said they did not want to spend the money on the ground to get it up to scratch, even when the lads amongst us who were builders offered to do the work.

We were angry as we were now obviously playing for a club with no ambition at all. So where did that put us, what would be the point in winning the league next year? In fact what would be the point of having a football club? Dad and manager Simon White resigned and were quickly meet by Steve Bailey who was local rival Street FC's chairman. Bailey offered the pair the management job at Street and within weeks we all left Glastonbury Town and followed dad and Simon. I felt sad to have left the club but what was the point in playing for a club that did not want to progress? It is very sad when I look at the club today. If we had got promotion and had spent a few quid on facilities, who knows where the club could have been? Possibly knocking on the Blue Square League now. But I will always have great affection for the club. Joining Street was also a difficult decision in itself, in terms of football. It meant dropping down three divisions, but we had a great set of lads who had been together years through our Glastonbury connections. Lads like Julian Coppell, Paul Skinner, John Tweed, Shaun Boobyer, Richard Smith, Martin Renton, Dougie, James Dash, Rob McCartney and Matt Harris. I want to give all those lads a mention as they were really important to me and still are. Within a few years, we had won various promotions and ended up in the Western League Premier Division.

I was now in my forties but I still had the love of the game. Football was like a drug to me. All the lads at Street were familiar as they were basically the Glastonbury side. I knew with my age that maybe manager Simon White may not pick me every week, but when he started to bring in a few strikers ahead of me, I found myself not even on the bench. I spoke to dad and told him how I felt and that lead to a meeting with Simon. I explained that all I wanted to do was play, and I knew that my playing career was getting shorter and shorter. And not being picked was getting more and more frustrating. So I decide to leave. Simon and dad were great about it and so were the lads. I think they all understood how I felt. I decided to keep myself fit while I looked for another club by training with my local side Wells City. They were a great bunch of lads and manager Johnny Russell was thrilled that I had wanted to train with them. After a few sessions he asked me if I would consider turning out for them. It was a no-brainer for me. Wells were my local club, and it sounds strange but it was great to meet up and get to know the people around where I lived. After all, Fil and I had lived in Wells for ages but I never really knew the people around me. It just felt right to join the local club. It certainly saved on petrol.

I have some great memories of playing for Wells City. I remember playing against local side Weston St John's. We played them three times in a season, with the cup and league fixtures. In those three games I scored 27 goals. That included 11 goals in one match against them. That one season I scored 52 goals – not bad for a 41-year-old. My reputation had always gone before me, although I never really had any problems with opponents trying to make a name for themselves by doing a ex-Bristol Rovers player. On the whole, after games they were really nice and would say things like; 'I can't believe I marked you, Paul. I used to watch you every Saturday'. But I do remember one game against a team called Cutters Friday FC. They were from South Bristol, which is basically the Bristol City side of Bristol. As we were warming up, this centre-half said to me; 'I'm going to kill you, Randall'. Now, I have been marked by some of the hardest footballers you could name, and in an era where they would stamp on you and it would be classed as a decent tackle. So the prospect of being man-marked by some spotty 20-year-old Bristol City fan never had me quaking in my boots. I thought I would have a bit of a laugh with him. He followed me all over the pitch. So when we had a corner I ran back to the centre circle. I'm blowed if he didn't follow me back there also. I stood there with my hands on my waist while his teammates were screaming at him to come back and defend. He got more and more embarrassed as he did not know what to do. I made his day complete when I left him for dead and scored in the second half. He never appeared in the clubhouse after the game although his teammates were pissing themselves over what I had done. I also remember, while I was playing for Wells, Fil had an asthma attack one night. I called the doctor and when he arrived she got worse so we called 999. They took her into the hospital at Taunton. I stayed to look after the kids. She was, thankfully, okay so on the Friday I called the hospital to speak to her, to see if it was okay for me to play against Saltford on the Saturday. She agreed so everything was fine. At this time, dad had joined the club as assistant manager. So I gave him my mobile phone that I had borrowed from work, so people could get hold of me if there was any problem with her while she was in hospital.

We were playing in Saltford and were 4–0 up. I had got two goals and was looking for my hat-trick, when my mobile rang and it was the hospital. They told dad that Fil had got worse and been moved to intensive care. Dad shouted from the touchline; 'Paul we got to go'. With that, I ran off the pitch, much to everybody's amazement. Dad and I jumped in the car and screeched off like two 1970s cops and headed to the hospital. Thankfully Fil had recovered and was home within days. It was a terrible shock but it's funny when I look back. I was in full kit with boots in the hospital. And typical of dad, he did phone Saltford to find out how the game ended.

I think, reading this book, you will see how important my dad has been to me over the years. He encouraged me throughout my career and he has given me advice; sometimes good and sometimes bad. He has always been there for me. He has watched nearly every game I have played in. I have been with Wells for around 15 years and they are a big part of mine and dads life. Mark came into the side as a 14-year-old and he played wide left. He's now a full-back and all left foot – Christ knows where that came from. We played together on numerous occasions in the first team, reserves and A-team. He is treated like one of the lads. I still get a feeling of enormous pride to see him play, and to do it with my own father stood next to me is very special. It's the same when I go and watch Kelly play netball for Wells Ladies. She has been very successful at the sport, winning promotions and cups. I am bursting with pride when I see them both doing so well at their chosen sports.

I have had some funny moments being involved in Mark's time at Wells City. I remember a couple of times when he was out on the wing. I was centre-forward and giving him a right old bollocking for not getting the right crosses into me. I also remember playing in a game at Frys in Keynsham when we were both substitutes. The manager made a double substitution. The ref came over and said; 'right Paul, I know who you are but what's your name, son?' To which Mark said; 'I'm his son'. I will never forget the look on the ref's face that day. Although the last couple of years of my career I turned into a bit of a journeyman as I looked to get settled somewhere, it's ironic that I became settled with the club that was on my own doorstep.

I gave up playing at 47 years old. I had a real knee problem. I remember sitting in the dressing room at half-time in a game with Weston St John. Funnily enough, I had missed a penalty. I told the lads my knee was shot, as it was throbbing with pain. With that, I just kicked the boots off and made the decision that playing was over for me. It certainly was for my knee, as now I have half a knee replacement. I still get the boots on for the odd charity game, and I have no regrets as I loved every minute as a footballer; even those days when I wasn't picked at Stoke or Rovers. The most important thing was that I had done what I always wanted to do, which was to be a footballer. To hang my boots up at my local club, Wells, seemed a perfect ending. Over the years I have seen Wells City grow and facilities get better and better, which in turn attracts better footballers to come to the club. Although I am still involved in coaching the lads, I always wonder if they could do with another forward. Even though he is in his 50s.

Chapter Twenty

Today

So this is it the last chapter of the book. I told you at the start it was not a birds, booze and gambling life – although I have had my moments. It was always going to be a story of family and never giving up, and I feel that's how my life has been.

Today I am still involved in football with Wells City as well as being the president of the club – a title that I am extremely honoured to have. I also help out with the first team in an assistant manager's role. Lots of people have asked me if I ever fancied being a manager, and when you look at the Rovers and Stoke dressing rooms, they certainly produced some great-calibre managers: Tony Pulis, Ian Holloway, Bobby Gould, Geraint Williams, Gerry Francis, Howard Kendall and Dennis Smith. But management was never for me; I don't think I could have been ruthless enough to do it properly. I don't have any regrets when it comes to football either. I know the game is full of what-ifs, and maybe if I had banged on a few managers' doors a bit more, I may have had a different career, but that just wasn't my style. I do think 'what if I had gone on loan to Howard Kendall's Blackburn Rovers when I was at Stoke City, or what if I had got on that plane to Holland when I was on my way out at Bristol Rovers'. But they are just passing thoughts – certainly not things that I would dwell on. I would not change a single moment of my career for anything. The supporters at all the clubs I have played for have been fantastic. They have taken to me, from the moment I signed for them, and the affection they have shown me after my career, whenever I have gone back, has been a humbling experience to say the least.

I remember getting a call from Bath City a few years ago. They told me that the supporters had a vote to name the new bar at the club and they had voted for it to be called Randall's. It was such a fantastic thing for them to do. I was invited with my family to the opening, where TV star Ricky Tomlinson was to help with the evening. Being a scouser, he hit it off with my family and it was a great night all round. It still makes me smile when I go past the ground and see the 'Randall's' sign up at Twerton Park. I have spent many a time in bars in my life but to have one named after me is a dream.

Bristol Rovers fans have also been very dear to my heart and they always will be. The people at the club always look after old players and that says a great deal about the directors. They are a special club. I was invited to a wonderful afternoon, which happened to fall on my 50th birthday. Rovers were playing Southampton in the FA Cup (what a perfect day) and I went to the game with dad as guests of the club. Director Geoff Dunford introduced me to Southampton's legendary ex-manager, Laurie McMenemy, in the boardroom. He shook my hand and said; 'I remember this bugger all those years ago'. We had a laugh and he was very complimentary about my ability in those days. Rovers won 1–0 with a goal from Rickie Lambert. As I was leaving the ground, every five or six steps I was stopped by Gas Heads wanting me to autograph things and have a drink with them. In the end, me and dad gave in and were taken to the supporters' bar, where I was suddenly handed a microphone and asked to say a few words to the fans. It was packed to the rafters. I stood up on a chair and you could have heard a pin drop. 'Well done today', I said, 'and let's hope we can go all the way. Remember, once a Gas Head, always a Gas Head'. With that, the place erupted in chants of 'Randall, Randall, Randall, Randall'; it was a perfect birthday present for me.

Another humbling experience was when I went to see Rovers at Wembley in the Freight Rover Final. I went with dad and two mates, Stuart and Dave. We parked outside of Wembley and caught the tube in; I had met a few Rovers fans on the way to Wembley and we had a great laugh. On arrival, we typically found the nearest pub, which was heaving with Gas Heads, and somebody spotted me as I went to the bar. The whole place started chanting my name. I then must have posed for hundreds of pictures for people. Things like that, and the outpouring of affection for me, are something that will stay with me forever. Why the Gas Heads took to me so much, I will never know. There have been far better players at the club than me, but I will always have great respect for them.

I have also experienced the warmth of fans in my day job. Today I work for the Glastonbury pharmacy as a dispenser, supplying all the local nursing homes around the area. It's a job I have done for over 15 years and I love every minute of it. It came about when I was working as a barman for Tor Leisure and playing at Bath City. I was sat in the bar with a few friends, putting the world to rights, when one of my mates, Malcolm Birks – himself a pharmacist – was saying how his firm needed a driver. I was starting to get cheesed off with the bar work and he arranged an interview for me at his firm. I went for the interview, where I met the boss, Dave Sanderson – who happened to be a Fulham fan. We talked football throughout the interview. I got the job and have been there ever since; rising up from van driver to dispenser. It's great when we get deliveries from drivers from the Bristol area; they look at me then look at the paperwork, then say; 'my God, it is you?' I have a real laugh with them, whether they are City or Rovers – I'm just very proud that they remember me.

So that's it, the end of the book. It started by recalling that terrible night of Vinny's death, and I hope reading the chapters you get a sense of what a close wonderful family I came from. I never gave up on my dream of being a professional footballer, and when it happened it gave me a wonderful lifestyle. But I never took any of it for granted. I always wanted to remain true to myself and those around me; just good old Punky!

The Dream Team

MARTIN THOMAS
BRISTOL ROVERS

PETER AITKEN	**MICKEY DOYLE**	**DENNIS SMITH**	**PHIL BATER**
BRISTOL ROVERS	STOKE CITY	STOKE CITY	BRISTOL ROVERS

TERRY CONROY	**HOWARD KENDALL**	**ALAN BALL**	**MICKEY BARRETT**
STOKE CITY	STOKE CITY	BRISTOL ROVERS	BRISTOL ROVERS

PAUL RANDALL   **DAVE STANIFORTH**
BRISTOL ROVERS   BRISTOL ROVERS

MANAGER – ALAN DURBAN
STOKE CITY

People always ask me who the best players I ever played with were. Well it's very difficult, but as Neil wanted me to put something down on paper, this is the team that I have come up with. I have not put subs down, as there would be too many to choose from, even by today's standards.

Martin Thomas – Martin was a brilliant 'keeper who had everything. Good at shot-stopping and crosses. Excellent attitude and a great trainer. You could always see that he would go on to play at a higher level and it's great to see him working with the England set-up today.

Peter Aitken and Phil Bater – Great full-backs. Peter was a great tackler and his timing was perfect. He was also a great lad to have in the dressing room. I'm sure he gave me the nickname Punky. Phil was quick and hard; you only have to see footage of the Southampton FA cup game to see he was Man of the Match, even though I got all the plaudits. When I arrived at Eastville, they both made me feel really welcome.

Mickey Doyle – He was real quality. He had been there and done it at Man City and Stoke City. He was fantastic in the air as well as on the floor.

Dennis Smith – When I first met Dennis, he was on crutches and had a black eye. When I played with him I saw why. He would give everything; he was hard as nails and was a brilliant defender who helped me when I arrived at Stoke.

Terry Conroy – Though coming to the end of his career, you could see his quality even then; he could find a pass without thinking.

Howard Kendall – A true great. You could see his first touch was amazing; and he would help you on and off the field. In training I could have watched him all day.

Alan Ball – Been there and done it; a real gentleman who read the game like a genius. It was a privilege to have graced the same pitch as him and something I won't forget.

Mickey Barrett – An absolute tragedy that he died so young. He had great pace and could turn on a sixpence, I'm sure Mickey would have played at the very top if not for his sad death.

Paul Randall – Of course I should be in the team, it's my book!

Dave Staniforth – My first real striking partner, who helped me immensely when I first joined Rovers. He would talk to me in games and always helped me in training. He played a big part in me getting the success I had at Bristol Rovers.

Manager Alan Durban – The only boss who bought and sold me. He was upfront and honest and he believed in me, even though he left me out of the side at times. I will always be grateful that he gave me a chance in the top flight.

Looking at the team, I wonder what they all might be worth in today's market. People often say to me, 'I bet you would like to play now, Paul'. Well I certainly would have liked the money. I don't resent the modern player getting what they earn; who wouldn't like that? But the modern player is detached from the average fan. That is the difference between the eras. I played in a time where you would sign stuff for kids without talking about image rights; it was a time when you would go to the local pub and chat to the fans. If they did not think you were doing it on a Saturday, they told you.

Referees have changed also; whether they are under more pressure today, I don't know; but I do know we used to have a chat and a laugh with them.

Certainly not chase after them, wanting a fellow player sent off. I know a lot has been made recently of players struggling to come to terms with giving up football. It was probably easier for my generation. You could earn more outside the game than in it. We just got on with retirement and found a job. We were never given any advice about how to cope with the real world. It's different for the modern players; many of them have been at academies since they were eight years old. They know nothing else but the game, so when it's had enough of them they struggle despite the money. It was different for me, as I was working full-time when I left school and knew what 'real' work was like. I watch a lot of games at lower level with Wells City, and it dismays me to see that there doesn't appear to be clubs out there looking for the next Paul Randall. If I was about today, I would not have been given a chance. Clubs would have looked at me and thought; 'If he's 19 and he hasn't been with a club, then he's probably not worth going to see'. That's the sad thing; you don't have to have been with an academy. Lads slip through the net and my advice to them is never give up; it can happen!

Testimonials

I first became aware of Paul Randall after reading in various newspapers that manager Alan Durban was interested in buying this new scoring sensation from Bristol Rovers. I was an established striker at Stoke City so obviously I was interested in him. Paul arrived at Stoke and came into what was an ageing side. He handled it really well and gained the respect of everyone due to the fact that he could play. He was lightning quick; very skilful and had great technique, which was unusual for a lad coming into the game late. When Paul signed, I was 27 years old and I had been thinking of going into coaching, so I would try and give as much encouragement to the youngsters at the club, like Paul, Adrian Heath, Paul Bracewell and Peter Fox. Paul was always willing to learn. Although I probably led him astray off the field if I'm honest. He did really well for Stoke City in his time there. He was very popular with the fans and he was very popular in the dressing room. He was a great teammate and friend, even if I couldn't understand him sometimes with that West Country accent.

Viv Busby
Stoke City 1977–1980

Paul Randall arrived at the Victoria Ground with a big reputation. As supporters, we were aware of his goal-scoring exploits for Bristol Rovers, and the moment he put pen to paper for us we knew we would get promotion to the top flight. Paul never let us down. I felt a bit sorry for him after our promotion, as he seemed to be in and out of the side. But we never heard him moaning in the press like some players do today. He was the ultimate professional for us supporters; he always came to fundraising events we had and always had time to chat. He will always be popular with the fans as he was part of our history with that promotion-winning side.

Mike Williams
Stoke City fan since 1969

Paul Randall will always be my favourite Rovers player. I remember him coming to the club. I was 11 years old. He was so exciting that the Eastville crowd roared when he got the ball. I remember playing football with my mates in St George's Park, Bristol, about 1978. The World Cup was on and all my mates were pretending to be Kempes, Rossi, Platini and Dalglish – not me. I was always Paul Randall. I think I cried when he left for Stoke City.

Peter Forman
Gas Head

I remember a game at Eastville in the 1978–79 season. We drew 5–5 and Paul got a hat-trick. He was awesome that day. I dread to think what he would be worth in today's market. He was a goalscorer. He had speed and great feet. I was only a kid when he left for Stoke City but when he came back, you could see he had become a better player. We should never have let him go to Yeovil as he still could have done a job for us.

Alan Drewcroft
Bristol Rovers fan for life

I have a lot of time for Paul Randall. He was great for us at Yeovil and when he left for rivals Bath City, me and my mates slaughtered him on his return to Huish Park. The ball went out for a throw-in and as he came towards us, we called him every name under the sun. He picked up the ball, smiled and said; 'You won't be buying me a beer later then, lads'. Everybody fell about laughing.

That was Paul; he never took himself too seriously and the fans loved him for it.

Andy Forbes
Yeovil Town fan since 1974

I first met Paul Randall when he came to Bristol Rovers for some games as a teenager. I was working with Bobby Campbell in the youth team when he arrived with his dad. Paul had great technique and a wonderful eye for goals, which he has never lost. Years later, when he joined the club in his second spell, I worked with him when I ran the reserves under Bobby Gould. His attitude was always first-class. I know he was upset about not being in Bobby's team but he just got on with it. I would talk to him and tell him that they could not ignore you if you scored goals and his record with the reserves was phenomenal. I loved having him with me in the reserves, as he was great with the other younger lads. When I became manager of Bath City in the 80s, Paul was at Yeovil Town and I desperately wanted to sign him. I knew that if I got him, we would get promotion. With Paul, you knew what you would be getting, and that was a terrific lad with a great attitude, plus that thing that every team needs – a goalscorer. He was a joy to work with and I dread to think what he would have been worth today.

Harold Jarman
Bristol Rovers legend 1959–1973

Looking back over the years, one player at Bristol Rovers was the diamond in the rough and that player was Paul Randall. A lad who came from non-league football and set the football league alight. When Paul joined the club, we were desperate for a goal-scorer as our two strikers, Alan Warboys and Bruce Bannister – AKA 'Smash and Grab' – had both left the club. Suddenly, a young, skinny lad walked into the dressing room from non-league football. I saw him play his first reserve game and he scored, but I never expected things to go as well as they did. He scored on his debut against Cardiff City. You only had to watch him to know he was a natural. As a kid I loved watching Jimmy Greaves, and Paul had that killer instinct that Jimmy had. He was ice cold in front of goal, and as a defender it was great to have that sort of player in the side. When we were up against it, we knew that if we got the ball up to Paul then he would get us a goal. As time went on, you could see Paul develop both physically and mentally. His confidence grew and grew but even though he deservedly got all the plaudits at that time, he was still the unassuming young lad he was when he joined. Paul lit up the changing room when he came to Rovers and he is a fine example to youngsters about not giving up on your dream. It was a pleasure to play with him and against him.

Peter Aitken
Bristol Rovers 1972–1980

I have two great memories of Paul. The first is watching him round the keeper as we beat Southampton in the FA Cup – a game I still watch on my video at home. Secondly, when I was standing in the open terrace watching Rovers against Liverpool in the FA Cup at Twerton Park and in front of me was my hero – AKA God – Paul Randall. It made my night to meet him.

Ned Cartwright
Bristol Rovers fan

I did not know much about Paul 'Punky' Randall when he came to Bristol Rovers. I had seen in the local paper that we were signing a lad from one of the local non-league sides, but to be honest I never paid much attention as we were always bringing in lads for trials. He came to us full of confidence, but not in an arrogant way, and he gave 100%, and that's why he fitted in with the lads and that's why the fans took to him. At that time, the club was looking for a hero and in Paul they found one. He was ice cool in front of goal and there was no one better in the whole country when faced with a one-on-one situation. His dad Ken kept his feet on the ground and he had a wonderful family behind him, and I'm sure that helped him settle with us. I shared many wonderful times with Paul over the years but one I would like to forget is the time we both decided to have our hair permed. Now I know this was the 1980s but there really was no excuse for it and it sends shivers down my spine just thinking of it. When I looked at myself in the mirror, I had gone from tough-tackling full-back to Shirley Temple! We both went into training together and got slaughtered by the lads. Paul just laughed along with them, taking it all in good part, whereas I shaved my head the next day. That was

Paul – he never took life too seriously and never took himself too seriously and that's how he played with a smile on his face. The fans loved him and his teammates did as well. He was a one-off.

Phil Bater
Bristol Rovers 1974–1981 / 1983–1986

When I look back over the many Rovers games I have seen – home and away since 1974 – I realise that I have seen Paul Randall score more goals for the world's greatest club than any other player. Many remember the youthful exuberance or the dark, flowing locks; the darting runs through the heart of static Division Two defences, or his presence in the six-yard box at corners. It was always blindingly obvious that Paul had goals in him and, tucked away in the underbelly of the old Eastville Stadium, watching the boys in the quartered shirts in action, it was evident that opposition defenders feared him too. Of course, there were more important or better-struck goals, but then I remember best a game at home against Preston North End in April 1983. All had appeared lost; Rovers trailing by a solitary goal at half-time, but the introduction of Archie Stephens as substitute lent an air of inevitability to Rovers' comeback. Archie, Mickey Barrett and of course, the one and only Paul Randall, with his 20th league goal of the season, scored the goals that gave Rovers a 3–2 victory and sent us scurrying back home, content.

Stephen Byrne
Rovers Fan

People in football talk about 'living the dream' and clichés like, 'making the most of your opportunities' – well, Paul simply did that. I had only just got in the Rovers team myself when Paul was signed from Glastonbury, and by the end of the week he had made his first team debut away to Cardiff City. The headline writers had a field day – '*Kid Randall's Supermarket Bargain Buy*' after he scored on his debut in a 1–1 draw. It was a Roy of the Rovers story. Paul had been working in a supermarket a week before, and here he was, hitting the headlines. The one thing that was evident from the start was that not only was he a natural goal-scorer, but he played on the shoulder of the last defender and was always a threat in behind. He had great pace and went 'cold' in front of the goal – by that I mean he had composure and did not panic. With us being the youngest in the team, we also became good mates off the pitch, and spent many a night celebrating a victory. It was a shame we lost him to Stoke City but from Paul's point of view it was an opportunity he could not turn down. Earlier in the 2012–13 season, I went back to Rovers for a game and Paul was there with his father, Ken. It was great to catch up after what had been nigh-on 25 years. I'm glad that Paul has put his story into words because it really was 'living the dream' and I'm sure it will be an entertaining read.

Martin Thomas
Bristol Rovers 1976-1982

I first met Punky when I went to Bristol Rovers in the summer of 1983. I had been released from Oxford United and was invited by Rovers manager David Williams to join them on their pre-season tour of Scotland. All the Rovers lads were great, especially Paul, who made me feel welcome with his West Country/ Scouse sense of humour. Unfortunately after the two-week tour of Scotland, it did not work out for me and therefore I joined Yeovil Town part-time, with the other half of my job in the commercial department. In the 85–86 season, Paul joined the part-time ranks of Yeovil Town from Bristol Rovers. The Yeovil Town manager at the time was former Bristol City boss Gerry Gow. Paul had a natural instinct in front of goal and certainly helped in our rise from the depths of non-league football. Paul lived locally, in Glastonbury, and was often accompanied by his father Ken, who is a truly larger than life character. Paul joined the commercial department and although he was good at his job, he decided it was not for him.

As with anything in life, time went on and I changed clubs and lost contact. However, I did meet up with Paul and his father Ken when Rovers played Yeovil at the Memorial Stadium. And it was an afternoon I will never forget.

Dave Linney
Commercial Manager – Yeovil Town FC

I signed Paul Randall from Stoke City whilst I was manager of Bristol Rovers. It was his second spell at the club and I wanted him for one reason, and that was due to the fact that he was a natural goal-scorer. I had played with Alan Clark and Jimmy Greaves, and when it came to putting the ball in the net, Paul was up there with the both of them. His pace was phenomenal and he had the ability to go with it. He was a great trainer and he never gave me any problems. A popular guy in the dressing room and a very positive lad to have around you, he had a big influence on the other lads. I was really pleased to get his signature for 'The Gas' and bring home a fans' favourite who never let anyone down.

Terry Cooper
Bristol Rovers Manager 1980–81

Paul Randall was one of those players who became local heroes. He played with a style and cheek that was communicated instantly to those watching. I remember once, at Bath City, he crossed from the touchline into the goalmouth, and the ball sailed over the 'keeper's head and into the goal. Was it a shot or a cross? Paul turned to the crowd; held out his arms as if to say it was intended. We loved him for it. So much, in fact, that the supporters' bar is called Randall's. As he said, he had been in many bars but never had one named after him. We shall drink to the great memories he gave us for years.

Ken Loach
Film Director and Bath City fan

Nowadays, if anybody said to you: 'We have a player that can score loads of goals but he is working in your local supermarket', you would laugh. Players now come through academies and get signed up when very young and then farmed out to lower league clubs. Paul Randall was truly a one-off; someone who escaped the net and found himself playing for his local club before Rovers stepped in and gave him a chance. Boy, he didn't let anyone down. In his first spell with Rovers, I remember as a youngster watching him play. He had the knack of a natural goal-scorer; he knew where the goal was and needed very few chances to score. Rovers could not believe how someone previously stacking shelves was now a hot property. Deservedly, Paul got his big move to Stoke City but still remained someone close to his roots, returning for a second good spell back at The Gas. The fella was, and is, a true legend! Nobody will forget those heady days watching The Gas and seeing Paul score. When you think of Rovers legends, names such as Warboys, Bannister, Cureton and Roberts come, but trust me: Paul Randall is right there amongst them. Thanks Paul, for the great memories.

Kevin Hurcombe
Gas Head

I remember being a 17-year-old lad playing in Yeovil Town's reserves when Paul was a well-established first team player. With what he had done in the game and the big money moves Paul had achieved, he certainly was no Big Time Charlie. It did not matter if you were a top first team player or a young lad in the reserves, Paul would treat you all the same. Paul being a bit of a local lad made him a firm favourite with the crowd, and he was always one of the last to leave the players' bar after a good chinwag with the supporters and a belly full of local brew. Mind you, I wasn't sure who was doing the most talking – Paul or his much travelled dad, Ken. Wherever you saw Paul, his dad would be right alongside him – a very likeable man in his own right. I remember Paul was recovering from injury once and playing in the reserves alongside myself – he told me to get the ball into the box and he would get on the end of it. He certainly did – scoring five goals that day. Paul was one of the most natural goal-scorers I have ever come across. It was a true pleasure to have played alongside him and to have watched him train. Paul will be remembered by the Yeovil Town supporters for the goals he scored and the quality he brought to the team.

Tony Pounder
Yeovil Town

I first met Paul Randall at Stoke City, where I was coming to the end of my playing career. Paul had come from Bristol Rovers and to be honest, we did not know much about him – only the fact that the 'gaffer', Alan Durban, had signed a goal-scorer. And that's exactly what he was, although not in the sense of a big target man. He was incredibly quick and his game was playing on the shoulder of the last man, and at that time he was second to none. Paul was technically a very gifted player which was surprising as he came into the game late. He was also a great lad to have in the dressing room. When I moved to Blackburn as Player Manager, I tried to get him on loan but it never happened – that's how highly I rated him. He is a very down-to-earth lad and I wonder sometimes if he realises just how good he was.

Howard Kendall
Stoke City 1977–79

While very much in the promotion hunt in the old Division Two at Christmas time 1978, Stoke City managed to escape with a 0–0 draw at Bristol Rovers. My two centre-halves should have still been in the top division, having had great careers and won league and cup honours. Denis Smith and Mike Doyle were uncompromising and experienced defenders. I sat with them on the journey home and asked them what their opinion was of the 23-year-old Randall, who sat top of the division's goalscoring charts with 13 goals. They confirmed what I had seen that day and on a previous visit to Eastville to watch Paul. Within a week I had signed Paul and he played regularly in our promotion side for the remainder of that season. Paul was quick, always on the move in the box and always looking for space between the full-back and the centre-back. Due to the rapid development of Garth Crooks, Lee Chapman and Adrian Heath, there was intense competition for the striker's position in the top league and Paul was asked to play wider than he would have liked in many matches the following season. This he did without complaint to help establish Stoke City in the top flight.

Winning promotion away on the final day at Notts County at the end of that first season remains one of the most memorable and satisfying days of my career. I'm glad Paul was part of that day and hopefully he enjoyed his stay in the Potteries as much as I did.

Alan Durban
Stoke City Manager 1978–81

Looking back now to 30-odd years ago when I would be watching Paul Randall play, in my capacity as HTV's commentator and the *Daily Telegraph* football writer for the South West, I have clear memories of a classy goalscorer. Paul was very good at the hard bit in football – getting the ball in the net. He had anticipation, could sense where the ball was going to arrive in the box – that half-second before other players. This gave him time. He also had great composure in front of the goal and would put the ball in the back of the net without even thinking. He figures in the memory recesses of this 79-year-old writer as being able to play with his head up when in possession. Therefore, he could decide what to do next and where. It all added up to a man who could score against high-class opposition – important goals like the Southampton FA Cup game. I was there commentating that day and it was a privilege to see a young, talented lad at the start of his career. Paul, you brought many memories to all who saw you and thank you for that.

Roger Malone
HTV Commentator/Journalist

Being the manager of a football club has many ups and downs. Putting a team together that gets success, giving young players their debut, and signing them up to a chance of a career are the best ups for me. I have memories of all of them from my time with Bristol Rovers. As a manager, you have scouts looking for talent all the time; you have meetings with your scouts and staff to discuss potential targets. With Paul, the decision to take him was a real no-brainer. Colin Dobson, who had done a brilliant job as a player and was now on the coaching staff, had set up a pre-season game against Frome Town. We had put together a team of players with some experience but mostly our youth team. Colin was in charge of the team and I went along to see how we got on. It wasn't long before I thought, 'Wow, who is that lad in the Frome team, running us ragged?' Half-time arrived and I went over to Dobbie, told him the lad could play and asked if he couldn't go out and find out some more about him. Was he a pro? Dobbie came back and said he wasn't – the lad worked in a supermarket. I told him we must have him at the club and not let the grass grow. I told him to have a word with the lad, to tell him we were impressed with him and would like him at Rovers, if that was what he wanted. I then went over to their management, who said, 'Yes, he's a good lad but we have just got him from Glastonbury. We won't stand in his way; just give us a few bob to help the club along'. I then set off to Bristol to see the Rovers chairman, who said, 'Sorry, at the last board meeting you were informed no more players as the finances are just not there'. I told him that this lad could be a diamond. 'You sign him and I will pay his wages', I said, 'But I get the transfer fee if a club comes in for him at a later date, and believe me, someone will come in for him'. The next day, the chairman phoned to say they'd pay his wages. The rest is in the history books.

Paul did well, right from the off. Sadly, we did not have many games together as I felt the club needed a fresh approach and I moved on to America. When you leave a club it's always nice to hear that the players you once managed are doing well. Watching and hearing about the goals Paul was scoring for Rovers, and then his move to Stoke City, made me immensely proud. Paul can be proud of what he achieved in the game but for me, what I have to thank him for most of all, is the buzz I felt the first time I ever saw him play.

Don Megson
Bristol Rovers Manager 1972–77

I write a regular column in the *Bristol Evening Post* on a Monday evening, where I try to recall amusing stories from my footballing career. Paul has probably appeared in quite a few of my columns over the years. I enjoyed a spell with Paul through the twilight of his career at Bath City. Obviously we all knew of him through his goalscoring feats at Bristol Rovers and Stoke City before joining the non-league team and our bitter rivals, Yeovil Town. In his first season at Bath City, he scored over 50 goals, and then 20 the following two seasons, before leaving to join Weymouth FC. He was a class act to play alongside and the goals he contributed helped the club to promotion. My memories of Paul or 'Punky', as he was known to his teammates, always bring a smile to my face. I have no doubt that if he was playing today and scoring like he did back in his heyday, he would command a transfer fee in the millions; easy.

I believe his transfer at the time to Bath City was the price of a sheepskin coat. The reason I say this is because he always seemed to wear one off the pitch. The first time I saw him wearing it, I had to look twice because I thought football commentator John Motson was coming towards me! My abiding memories of Paul usually refer to him returning to the club to start pre-season training after the summer break. Paul was known to pile on the pounds when not in training; he had a job to keep out of chip shops and pubs! I can remember him standing on a set of weighing scales in the club's changing rooms, when I spotted him sucking his stomach in and looking down. I shouted; 'that won't make you look lighter, Paul'. He replied; 'I know but it's the only way I can see the dial on the scales'.

I know that Paul has a similar sense of humour to me, as he loved some of the silly jokes I used to share with him. On one occasion after training, we walked down to the local shops. We walked into a fishmonger's, where I asked the assistant if they made fishcakes. He nodded and said they did, so I replied, 'can I have one; it's my goldfish's birthday today.' We both walked out laughing, leaving the assistant shaking his head. Although Paul had many supporters, his biggest was his dad, Ken, who he is very close to. He respected his advice in football and in life in general. Likewise, I am very close to my dad and I can remember telling Paul about the advice my dad gave to me. He said, 'Son, always fight fire with fire.' Which is probably why he got thrown out of the fire service. Just to conclude, Paul was a great goal-scorer, who worked hard for the team, and he is a person I have always looked up to.

Dave Payne
Bath City 1983–91

I remember working on a building site and hearing the news that manager Gerry Gow had got Paul Randall from Bristol Rovers. As a lifelong Yeovil Town fan, I could not believe that Rovers had let him go. It was also a surprise that no league club had come in for him. He gave the whole club a lift when he joined and he will always be the one person I loved to go and see in a Yeovil shirt – he will always be a top man!

Peter Wishton
Yeovil Town Fan

I remember the Severnside derby against Bristol Rovers – they were always tasty affairs against our rivals from over the River Severn. Apparently, Rovers had a young lad up front who was making his debut, called Paul Randall. To be fair, he looked about six stone, wringing wet, and I thought, 'Well, I'll give him a bit of a dig early on to welcome him to league football.' That was the plan anyway. I never got near him for most of the game. He was devastatingly quick and managed to score – even if it did come off his shin. Paul was a true goalscorer and I enjoyed our tussles together. I have played against many great players over the years, but that was certainly one of the greatest debuts I have ever seen.

Phil Dwyer
Cardiff City 1972–85

I used to go to a lot of the Rovers games with Paul. He wangled it so that I could just walk onto the pitch and join in with the other professional photographers and snap away (it was better than paying to go in). One time I had to have a very minor operation on my 'rear end' and told Paul that I wouldn't be able to make the following week's game, which was a shame as it was the City and Rovers derby match. On the Saturday, the doctor said I could leave the hospital. I didn't have time to phone Paul so I just turned up and took my usual position behind the goal, camera in hand. The game was well into the second half and Rovers had a corner. Paul was stood in the six-yard box, waiting for the ball to come across, when he glanced down and saw me there. 'Titch', he said with a big smile on his face, 'how's your arse?' The look on the City defenders' faces was priceless!

David Titchener
Photographer and Friend

Paul Randall came to live in Glastonbury Somerset in 1961 and has become a firm favourite and cult hero in sporting circles. He is also a true and close friend.

I remember Paul as a six-year-old who came to watch Morlands play cricket at Glastonbury with his father, Ken, and despite the fact we were arguably the outstanding cricket side in Somerset with such players as Graham Burgess,

Peter (Dasher) Denning, Colin Atkinson and Brian Lobb – all Somerset County cricketers – Paul would get bored after two overs and concentrate on kicking his football.

At that tender age, Paul looked a natural. One of my favourite sayings on the cricket pitch has always been 'never known to drop a catch', but that was all to change whenever Paul was at a game. Sadly, my concentration levels dropped for a time, as I always had one eye on the footballing skills of this youngster. Peter Spiring, who was to play for Bristol City and Liverpool for a short spell, was also an up-and-coming prospect at more or less the same time, and it was ironic that the two talents should come from Glastonbury. Paul was different in the fact that he was an okay cricketer, but as a footballer he was a unique talent who had an eye for goal at such an early age. So many youngsters, when they get to a certain age, are inclined to let other matters have more importance in their life, but you always felt that with Paul's father Ken, this would not happen and football would always be the most important factor of all.

Goals on a regular basis for Glastonbury became the norm and following the switch to Bristol Rovers after trials at Bristol City and Manchester City, Paul Randall's name was becoming increasingly well-known in the mid-Somerset area. I remember when Paul made his debut with Bristol Rovers – we did not have a game at Glastonbury on that day and I sat in the kitchen listening to the commentary on the radio. I think it was Roger Malone who came through with the news that Paul had scored on his debut for Rovers against Cardiff City at Ninian Park. Paul became that cult hero from Glastonbury and I remember going to Eastville to watch the Rovers play a great Spurs side that included Glen Hoddle, and although Spurs won the game 3–2, it was Paul who had put Rovers in front after 15 minutes.

Glastonbury is a small community that houses around 10,000 people, but the entire area was suddenly put on the map in a much bigger way by the arrival of Paul Randall – who knew where the back of a football net was. Paul had a huge following despite moving to Stoke City – he would still return to his roots on a Saturday night at the local nightclub in Glastonbury. Yeovil Town, Bath City, Clevedon Town, Weymouth, Street and Wells City all had the opportunity of seeing Paul carry on his scoring feats – despite an old friend of both of ours, Ashley Hayne, saying that Paul should call it a day. Paul responded by playing against Weston St Johns three times in a month and scoring 21 goals in those three games. As they say, there was life in the old dog, despite being 43 years old. I had the fortune – or even misfortune – of playing alongside Paul during several Sunday morning games back in the 90s. Being a former goal-keeper and now playing upfront with a local legend was never easy, or at least not all of the time. Paul would set up so many opportunities for me to score in the first half and I did get a few tap-ins, but against the better clubs he would win the games on his own.

We now play cricket together for a team called the Travelling Wrinklies – the name's a giveaway – with Paul is the youngest player in the side. We also play in the same skittles team together called Cross Doubles. Paul is once again a natural. But there is also a certain amount of luck playing the game, which in some ways is similar to ten-pin bowling, although this game is made up of nine wooden pins. If Paul is unlucky he will stand and look at the rest of us with arms aloft, as if to say, 'what's the point?' and every time it happens now, in unison we all say with arms aloft, 'what's the point?' and that has become a cult saying for everybody. Paul is and always will be a true friend and a man you could never fall out with; if you did you would have to question your cred-ibility as a human being. We have had and always will have a special bond and Paul, being a proud person, is very much part of Wells Football Club, as Assistant Manager and also president of the club. But at the same time, Paul is very much a family man and has no greater pleasure than watching his two very talented children Mark and Kelly play football and netball respectively.

Statistics

		APPS	GOALS
BRISTOL ROVERS	1977–78	31	20
	1978–79	22	13
STOKE CITY	1978–79	20	5
	1979–80	16	1
	1980–81	8	2
BRISTOL ROVERS	1980–81	15	3
	1981–82	37	12
	1982–83	41	20
	1983–84	32	6
	1984–85	43	18
	1985–86	17	2
YEOVIL TOWN	1985–86	14	7
	1986–87	39	17
	1987–88	65	25
	1988–89	38	18
BATH CITY	1988–89	8	6
	1989–90	68	51
	1990–91	49	22
	1991–92	53	26
	1992–93	39	7

WEYMOUTH	NO RECORDS
CLEVEDON TOWN	NO RECORDS
WELTON ROVERS	NO RECORDS
GLASTONBURY TOWN	NO RECORDS
STREET	NO RECORDS
WELLS CITY	NO RECORDS